OF CHINA AND OF GREECE

Other Books by Greg Kuzma

Sitting Around (1969)
Something At Last Visible (1969)
Eleven Poems (1971)
The Bosporus (1971)
Harry's Things (1971)
Poems (1971)
Song for Someone Going Away and Other Poems
(1971)
Good News (1973)
What Friends Are For (1973)
A Problem of High Water (1973)
The Buffalo Shoot (1974)
The Obedience School (1974)
A Day in the World (1976)
Nebraska—A Poem (1977)
Adirondacks (1978)
Village Journal (1978)
For My Brother (1981)
Everyday Life (1983)
A Horse of a Different Color (1983)

Of China and of Greece

Greg Kuzma

NEW YORK

Acknowledgements

Some of these poems have appeared in the following publications, occasionally in earlier versions: *Prairie Schooner, New England Review, Konglomerati,* SUN, *Midwest Quarterly, Memphis State Review, Orpheus, The Sandhills & Other Geographies, The Carolina Quarterly, Socialist Review,* and *Brother Songs* (Holy Cow! Press).

Printed in the United States of America

First Edition

Library of Congress Cataloging in Publication Data

Kuzma, Greg.
    Of China and of Greece.

    I. Title.
PS3561.Up035   1984   811'.54   84-16365
ISBN 0-915342-43-X

The publication of this book is supported by grants from the National Endowment for the Arts in Washington, D.C., a federal agency, and the Ludwig Vogelstein Foundation.

To the memory of George P. Elliott

CONTENTS

OF CHINA AND OF GREECE

China and Greece

for Richard Eberhart

I saw the bee in the window.
And there was St. Cecelia in her rags
and there was Marshall Clarke at Almadoor.
One day I chanced upon the fly
fallen along the windowsill.
And the fields of Russia were full
of their winter still
and plump Napoleon warm in his furs.
August is a hard month here
the flowers will die for want of water.
Hitler strolled on his patio
and the drunk killers of Caesar
lay down by the purple lake.
Today in his garden the butterfly
with orange and black wings
settled on my hand.
The dust of centuries, goats' milk,
and Christ come barefoot among
the Pharisees.
A phone call last night about 10:30 from Ed Ritz
near Philadelphia.
A child born unto him and Madeline
arrives home.
Meanwhile the tribes of Borneo
send their old people
down river on rafts
and the river is full of crocodiles.
How are you doing, Ed, I
asked him.
In Minnesota, the northern lakes,
the harvest of the wild rice is
occasioned by the large consumption
of both beer and coffee.
Yesterday Mark brought a new friend to our house
a sickly looking boy, hair blond,
whose father owns half the town.
In Crete where we live
there are few dairy cows.

TVs are sold at three different
locations. Atilla the Hun
kept many dogs, all of which
were buried with him after
he sickened. Today in the
window the hummingbird has come
even though the center
of the moneyed world has shifted
from London to New York.

I sit in the kitchen tonight
and the world is mine.
Like Frank Jerosko of Jerosko's Lumber Company
in Rome, New York, whose son graduated
from high school with me, I have had
a good year. The cries
from the street do not bear
in them the cries of the dying
in the cancer wing of the
Lincoln General Hospital. I look
at a blooming zinnia, a whole
row of green ones, and my kidneys
stop aching. Who has gone
into the night with the news
of the battle. In what back
rooms are the betrayals taking place
which will deprive my children of
a sense of an expandable future,
good wool sweaters, or a cheap
funeral? Another star will
be visible tonight in the black sky,
just as in East Prussia bakeries
have stopped offering certain cheeses
in their cakes. Oh, Teresa,
still you should sing your song.
The groundhog slumbers in a heap
of dust, and Richard
Eberhart will be dust too.

It is winter.
The resorts in the south are flourishing.
Estelle Bradshaw has breathed her last

in a nursing home near Miami.
From Florida they sent her ashes.
Outside my door there is no snow
just as in the Sears Roebuck Company
of Albuquerque New Mexico
they have run out of air cleaners
for lawn mowers model #L8 7364 GH 9.
Pheasants were seen this morning
by one Lumir Fictim.
The President declares, from his office,
a measure of an agreement.
In the window the three snowmen
seem to have melted down
to their teeth and hats.
My mother's face is nearly all freckles.
In my case my waist is smaller
than it was last year,
and when I go into the hardware store
inquiring of bolts,
they seem to know me there, allow
me to write a check.
Over a book I see Galileo
squatting to piss, over his shoulders
the night sky nearly wrapped tight
by a window.

Now Columbus comes
over the water like a swan.
The year is 1856.
Baseball is not yet invented.
The Mescalero Apaches love their women.
In Central Park
a number of poets have gathered for a
reading. In the crowd
the man who will shoot a president
eats a cold pizza.
The price of the routine motor work
needed in order to maintain the
warranty on my car was $118.56.
Cedar City Utah has no
respectable camera shop.

I keep expecting a letter from you.
I keep thinking, somewhere,
that we shall meet.
Or maybe something of yours
will touch something of mine.
Perhaps on a shelf, far from here
or where you are,
a radio you owned
will share its dust with a
fork with which tonight
I bring to my lips
clean wedges of lettuce in
cheese sauce.
Perhaps my car will pass yours
going on a long journey.
And I will remember that red
and the plush upholstery.
Your face, if it is a woman's face,
stay with me down the road,
and in a dream some night
you'll serve me coffee at a
bar and grill. Or you will deliver
my infant son. Write. Or call.
There was a bull moose pictured
in a photograph. A man with
a big belly
has told me about Alaska,
a woman who has not healed
after having her first child
insists on playing a kind of
pinochle no one can find
the rules for.
Perhaps we will meet
or our children will
fall in love
and in some nearby church
inherit a life of toasters
and sticky linoleum.
Are there flowers in bloom now
where you are?
From your window can you see
the rain cutting the bright street open
showing the dark street.

Even after I am gone to bed
I sometimes have to get up
and go to the kitchen
there to eat a sandwich
and a glass of milk, the night
precariously dark.
Sometimes in the night
I have strange dreams,
but in the morning, when
I get up, usually I am happy
with the prospect of my work.
Is something similar your situation.
Did your father, uncle,
mother, expect, of that last trip,
other surprises. Today
in the window
a wren was taking a lengthy twig
into a wren house. Two jays sat
in the branches of a big tree.
And all the time a movie director
consulted a woman's breasts.
Twilight had at last fallen
over the Rappahannock Valley.
From the back yard, over
the sound of the radio,
my children's voices detail
another fading moment.
On the counter two leaves
and a shoe, dirt flaking
from its corrugated sole.
My father has gone
out into his living room,
and turning himself sideways
to the window, snaps off
the lamp switch with
the fingers of his left hand.

Sometimes

I am afraid of being crushed in the pincers
of an enormous dog. I am afraid of
breathing into my lungs the gastric juices
of my own stomach. I fear that the semi-trailer truck
will suddenly blow a tire and come swerving into my own lane
and turn my car and my body into a horrible pulp.
I am afraid it will not be quick enough when it happens.
I am afraid as well of lingering dying, living at the
edge of a cliff and the long hurt ache up the arms,
the bowels distended out through the anus, or the
lungs growing feathery and faint, crinkling up like
wax paper after the sandwich is removed.
I am afraid, at night, sometimes, of arising from bed
and smashing my shin on the weight set bar I have on
the floor by the edge of the bed, of the bone bruising,
and the lump rising up.
I am afraid of the fall down stairs, with the back
bone trying to right itself, the head trying to get
pointed in the right direction, but the body falling
like a child into a pool relaxed on a hot day,
only the arms breaking off in the posts of the railing.
I am afraid of having my skull crushed under the plate
of an enormous press which someone is lowering
a fraction of an inch at a time, of the skull cracking
first like a walnut shell, and the momentary relief,
of the eyes growing milky and then popping out,
staring back up briefly upon the twisted face, the
teeth pinned against each other, the splintering,
the facial bones breaking through the skin like a
wrecked ship coming up from the placid bottom
where all these years its rigging was a place for fish
to swim through, and the blood of course and the
squirting brains. I am afraid as well even to
look upon such things happening to others, afraid
to get out of the car at the roadside last week
when the big green pickup truck went over on its side,
and there was inside the cab the person jumping up and down
trying to get out, like a frog in a jar. I am afraid
of the fingers of cancer touching touching, or
pneumonia which floods the lungs with phlegm, or

the coughing fit which brings the stomach up, the tubes
to the back of the throat. I am afraid of the stench
of the body, the little whisps from the anus, the
gagging gargle breath of the old. I am afraid
that someday in front of a building someone will jump
upon me and snap my back like a twig and I go jostling
to the ground, dancing, jerking in a kind of sexual spasm.
Or that a knife will be inserted under my left breast
and like a zipper drawn across my chest while someone
says, as in the film "The Godfather," this is for you my friend.
I am afraid for the big soft belly I hide under shirts,
that it will be ripped open and the insides yanked out
and burned in front of me as used to be done nearly every week
or so in other civilized cultures. I am afraid for the ribs
that they will not be strong against the huge priers,
and that the heart will shrivel like a prune at a single touch.
I think of myself often on line with the beeves
waiting to be stuck or jabbed with the current,
the brain to sizzle up suddenly like a toaster short circuit,
and the whole body, once so quick and light, to fall like a
bag of mud onto the slimed floor. Or to do that
to other living things, to hook them and lift them
dazed onto a belt of bodies, to slice them open like butter
with hot knives, to peel them like bananas. I am
afraid that a bullet will come like a jet plane
right up the front of my face, right up a nostril
and take out the whole back of my skull and its contents,
and that it not be quick enough. Or that I might be
even in some dream impaled on a stake, feeling it rise
up through my rectum, up beside the lungs and out around
the left shoulder, and my hands bound and numb.
Or of having my throat ripped out by some vicious dog.
I am afraid that my hands will be hacked off by a big man
wearing a lumberjack shirt, first the left hand
and then the right, and that I will be then asked
to walk all the way home, looking down at my arms
and out again at the world, the butterflies, the lawn sprinklers
spinning their little silver cornets.

Piano

to Jackie

I look at my daughter
and think she should have a piano
that she should learn to play.
I foresee in the future rainy days
or too long evenings, in summer
after school is out, when the
drowse of the evening may
depress her, when, in the upstairs
mirror, putting up her hair, she
will feel painfully alone.
Wouldn't a piano be better than
all this walking about
trying to amuse ourselves?
On evenings lately we set out
riding our bikes or walking
past this or that or another door
staring with bemused faces into
this that or another yard.
We wave at carrots, admire,
turning to each other, a proper
green blue manicure, or a man
after work, stripped to his shirt
out hosing down a patch of
noisy weeds. Isn't it hopeless,
and wouldn't a piano be nicer?
She could go, for instance,
up to her upstairs room to pout,
to stare at her hands in the
late light, to pound them
between books, hoping to extend
her reach. She could take
long walks by herself—seeing nothing,
each face she met a keyboard,
strange notes winking away at
the corners of mouths. At breakfast
what a blue and bereft look
she would give the bowl of
rudely scrambled disorderly eggs.
And the years, how painfully they'd pass.

The day they would bring the piano
what an occasion, the dog
nipping at the workmen's feet,
the big crate coming up the walk
on short but stocky rolling pins—
a piece of ancient Egypt in a box,
and the legs last, carried by a
smiling man spitting on the lacquer.
Black, it would be black
it has to be.

All month the sun would shine
and she would play
tunes to the sun.
By moonlight she would draw
the thing in the piano
up out of the great harp.
Oh how her hands would sing
over the keys, how my heart
would be distracted, the days
she could not play, from flu or
disaffection, empty like a concert
hall in which the piano is away
having its teeth worked on.

Everyone I think should have a piano.
And not just a figurative piano.
But an actual piano.
Nothing is as actual as a piano.
A great black lug of a thing
or one in a new pink mist
glassily antiqued,
on which to set down pots full of
geraniums.
Imagine seeing her there
years later, eleven again,
her big front teeth drying out
over the black keys,
and your ears feeling like
beaten drums. Isn't it all
too much to have missed—
how to go on year after year
never having experienced it?

I see her now as she walks
out, green bathing suited, onto
the high diving board at the
Southern Utah State College swimming pool.
The pool below her is full
of rampaging pianos, some with
their great lids up.
A huge silence fills the room
there is the sound of
water lapping at the walls.
There is the sudden overprint
of hundreds of uplifted piano
keyboards.
And then this fair haired girl,
girl of the slender legs and
wrists, raises her hands
to play.

My daughter has those slender hands and ankles.
In a bathing suit she looks just
like she plays the piano, or did,
or should. Or nights when I
pass her room, her sleep so mild,
so undisturbed. Awaking as she
does each day refreshed. How can
she ever come to live in the
real world, without it,
the dark great ship, the unholy
combatant? Doesn't she need
this thing of an early failure?
How will the fine wood of her
soul take on its proper
seasoning?

What will she do, for instance, when
waiting for a date
he does not come at the
prescribed hour?
The dormitory is packed with
gradually depleting girls,
in ones or twos sucked out
sailing through spinning doors—

the sky dim with clouds.
Only the fat desk girl,
the one who keeps the alibis
and reads, each hour, the
grim clock face, and whose
study tonight is calculus—
water leaking out of a punctured
water can—
will seem to notice her,
sitting alone, hands folded and
numb in her lap like refugees.
There in the corner the
old piano, veteran of many such
nights, sits dumb and unexplored.
How much better it would be
to not just sit there on the couch,
alone, pianoless, the room a
crummy grocery store of groans.
Get up dear Jacquelyn and play!
Make the tardy boy sit down and wait
while you do Mozart, Beethoven, Brahms.
Show him that there's something
in your hands
which you can put there when he's not around.

Oh to play the piano.
Oh to have a daughter take lessons.
Minding the expenses, measuring in
like invisible sugar, the great and
future benefit. One eye always
on the clock we live
like the fat desk girl at
the dormitory,
always we push up steep front walks
great pieces of Egypt
to other houses.
How much better to be at home
listening to someone we love
play Tchaikovsky
or Chopin.
Or sit in the middle morn
over the scrambled eggs

a long face come to the table
to match our own,
to place on her thin small hand
our old and nail chewed ones,
to welcome her new sad self
amidst that special circle of ourselves.
Our eyes meet:
in every one a huge piano
spreads through blue or green or brown.
How empty is a life
without its music in it.

The Human Condition

1

He put on top of the other
until there was a large stack
carefully balancing each in turn
up to the point where the stack became precarious
then he started another stack
and proceeded in the same manner.
Then there was an earthquake killing him.

2

The Incas were great road builders.
As the Empire expanded the roads were extended
and one could say that the Empire
could not have expanded without the roads.
All parts of the Empire, even the most remote places,
were joined to all other places because
of the roads. When Pizarro arrived
he marched his small army
up along the coast over the marvelous
roads and into the cities of the Incas
and destroyed them.

3

My father fell from a building
and broke his eardrum in his left ear.
All of his life subsequently
he only half heard the world
or that the world he heard
did not exist or was lame like himself.
Gradually he thought of the world
as lame, and expected thereby
very little from it. He learned to content himself
with small things, or things which never
asked to be loved. Gradually he became
content.

4

I look at myself in the mirror and I ask
what is the matter with you, you
in the mirror? But what is the matter

with me does not appear in the
mirror. In the mirror I look secure
and happy. I am wearing a blue shirt.
I am wearing a red tie neatly over the
blue shirt. Someone has ironed my tie.
My face is washed. My eyes from a
full night's sleep are clear. There is no
evidence of the terrible dreams
which have disabled me.

5

My father spent many years and many dollars
on a gun collection. He bought
many guns, and would sit, sometimes,
in his room and take them out
and hold them. Who knows what
he imagined holding them. People
probably thought—Oh what a good
thing to have guns in the house, and
a man who knows how to use them,
in case a robber someday would
break in. But when the troubles came
they did not come from the outside
but from within the house, and what
they were no bullets could kill.

6

For years and years my wife was
unhappy and yet I was happy. For
years and years I worked to be
happy and I was happy, while all the
time my wife was unhappy. Now
that my brother is dead and I am
unhappy and cannot think of being happy,
she is happy and content with herself.
Probably the average amount
of happiness in our house has
not changed. Probably someone
looking at us from outside will
conclude that nothing has changed.

7
My brother worked for a whole year
on his motorcycle. It had gone to
pieces and needed much work. His
intention was to restore it as nearly
as possible to its original condition.
So that it would go 120 miles an hour.
Mother always said Jeff's going to kill
himself on that bike. Finally he
got the bike done. It was very lovely.
But it would go only 90 miles an hour.
Some compression had been lost in
the cylinders. A week after he finished
the rebuilding he killed himself driving
a car. Someone who saw Jeff go by in the car
claimed that the car was going 120 miles an hour.

8
My mother was an only child.
When she was very small her father
deserted her mother. Thereafter
her mother was a gloomy and sad woman.
She did not remarry.
Then my mother married and
I was born. For 8 years
I was an only child, and then
my brother was born. My mother
told me that my father did not
want children. Then I went off to
live by myself.
Then my mother left my father
and went to live by herself.
As her mother had lived by herself.
Then I married. Then my children
were born and grew.
Then Jeff died. Then I was
an only child, a father, a husband.

9
A man works hard and has a dream.
At night he falls asleep exhausted
and wakes up refreshed in the morning.
A woman works hard and has a dream.

At night she falls asleep exhausted
and wakes up refreshed in the morning.
They are married. They live
in the same house. They spend most
of their time together. They go
everywhere together. But they
do not have the same dream.

10
A man who thinks the world
conspires against him cannot be
at peace. A woman who thinks
the world is amused with her
but only if she is witty and clever
cannot be at peace. These two
people marry and live together for 25
years, struggle and groan, fight to
survive separately and also
together, maintaining against great odds
their unique views of reality.
Finally they separate and live apart.
The world takes no notice.

11
Ten years ago I moved from
the place I was born to the
Midwest, to the very center of the
country, and nestled there,
secure from the dangerous coasts.
Nothing could get to me.
Weather started elsewhere, and
gave fair warning.
The great events, the rises and falls,
occurred elsewhere. I sat
still and warm in my house—like dough—
rising gently into a round brown loaf.

12
I say to myself You have not been a good man.
I say to myself—which is worse—
You are not a good man, you have
not ever been a good man. I look around
me at others, to see what they are,

but I cannot see them for myself,
and even if I could see them,
I would not trust myself,
so little do I trust myself.

13

Every year at Christmas or at my brother's birthday
I would hesitate, I would not send him
anything. He is not ready yet, he is
not ready to be taken in, for him
the conventions do not work, do
not hold meaning. What could I send
him that he would need? What could
I buy for him that would not show off
that I have money and he does not?
I do not want to make him feel
he must reciprocate, he who has
no money. Then in September of 1977
he goes out and buys himself a huge expensive
accident.

14

Everyone I know and have loved
wants more and more.
I want five books of poems and three
books of essays. My father wants
two camping trailers, five fishing poles,
3 expensive shotguns. Mornings I
give up the sun to write a poem to
take up 9 pages in a book. Evening
my father gives up the stars, the
wind from the north, to add another
picture frame to his collection.
My wife collects furniture
my son saves plastic rockets
my daughter wears one after another
new dress, throwing them on the floor.

15

Leaves everywhere, the lawn suffocating.
So we rake the leaves. March
becomes April. We set the piles

of leaves on fire. It is sunset,
the day is ending. The smoke rises,
obscuring the sun. My eyes water,
my throat grows hoarse,
so that the grass which is ugly
and costly will be green at the
proper time.

The Room

It is with you. It is as it was.
It is the same, yet it is new.
What you had left returns,
yet what you had never felt
also is present.
Also there is another presence.
But you are not aware of it.
So it goes, all through the morning.
So you seem to be starting out,
and so you have grown in magnitude
taking upon yourself yourself
something of what you had been
and had perhaps forgotten.
So you seem to be enlarging
all through the morning.
It is nine o'clock.
And now it is ten o'clock.
Now you are bigger than you were before.
Now you are more than that.
Also with you
there is another presence.
Perhaps you will sense it.
Perhaps you have already
taken it into yourself.

It is the same with me.
It is what I was.
It has come back, a bit
of it, not all,
for how would all that fit?
Now I am here.
I too feel it, it is near,
now it touches. Now it goes
off, away from me,
transforms the chair. Now
it has come to fill it.
Now it beckons me.
There is light in the room.
But it is not the light.
There is a wall of dust
which rises through the light.

But it is not this.
Now what it was fades.
I feel it go out of me.
I am less. I start.

Yesterday I think it was I saw you.
Did you see me?
Yesterday I dreamed of me
walking somewhere, meeting you,
going with you somewhere.
Did you have a similar dream?
Yesterday I dreamed of you
dreaming of me, thinking of me
dreaming of you. Oh but alas
now it is today, it is here
but I do not see you,
neither do I hear your steps.

Was that you I saw
this morning as you crossed the room?
There was a sound, another,
there was a movement, a breathing
near me. I turned, I turned my eyes
in the direction of the sound,
seeing a glimpse of something,
seeing what seemed to fill me
to gladden me.
I sat there, I was glad.
It seemed I had always been glad
that I had always sat there.
And that you had crossed,
once, twice, years ago, that
you would come back. That
I would see you, that you
were also glad, that even now
where you have gone, you are
returning from that, that you are
starting out, that you are
on the way.

You have been on my mind.
Often I think of me,
but lately I think of you.

Something about you, something
I never noticed, something which
even I can see and cherish.
Is it yours, does it
belong to you, or is it
that, looking as I do, for more,
looking as I do for something to
settle for, something to discover,
I endow you with it,
you who already are so much.

Now comes a slow time in the chair.
This room, what can I say of it.
It is here, it has always been here.
The chair turned part way round.
The light in the corner.
Now it has crossed the floor.
Now it is on the wall.
Now it has left the corner.
If I could turn further.
If I could only shift from here
a little more
a little
perhaps I would see more of the light.

Last night a terrible dream.
I was here, as before.
I was where I am, and who
I am. I was in the chair,
and the chair where it is.
There was the light, where it is,
where it was,
and I could not see the light.
I knew it was there,
but I could not turn.
The chair held me.
Gladly did I hold the chair.
And the room where it was
around me.
Then I was out of the room.
Then I saw where the light is.
It was all around me.
All around the chair.

I was glad for the light.
I was glad for the chair.
But oh I could not see the room.
I was glad for the light,
and for the chair
but oh I could not see the room.
Help me, mother of God,
help me, you who pass in your blue clothes,
help me, you who are in the room.

I think I will write you
or I will write of you.
Perhaps you know already
all I will say.
But so much the better for that.
So much the better that you should know,
that we should both know
all I will say.
Perhaps I will not have to say
all I will say.
Now that you know,
now that I know that you know,
this is how I will start.
Like this, with these words:
"Here I am, thinking of you."
"Here I am, dreaming of you."

A dark day, you are gone.
The chair is desolate,
the room full of silence.
Where the light was
still it remains,
but calls out to me the more so,
such affrontation,
such dismay.
The room the same
and everything,
everything you were and are
a vapor now.
The day dark. The room. The chair desolate.
The day begun anyway.

Strange how we are never empty
entirely, entirely.
Strange now that you are gone
and the room echoes that.
How I, shrunk down in the chair,
seem another room,
a shrunken room
with a small light.
Still strange, that as I empty out
I fill.
Something is come in your place.
Something not you and yet you.
Fills me.
All day I have felt it
and the night before.
It is as if you are here.
It is as if you had not gone.

A night of dreams
followed by a day of dreams.
First I saw you as you had been.
Then in another place.
Then it was that you were gone
and I had but this to think about.
Then you were there, but new,
as if we had just begun.
It was a day long ago.
There was the chair, and
there was the light.
There was a movement,
something I had not seen.
It crossed. It crossed
the room, holding back the light.
Then there was the light.
And then I woke.
Then I woke up into dreams.
And what were these dreams?
What did I dream in them?
I dreamt of you.
I dreamt of you here.
I dreamt of you standing in light.
I dreamt that you and the light
were one.
That you had become the light.

It is nine o'clock in the room.
The light wavers.
It is ten o'clock in the room.
The light grows steady on the wall.
It is eleven.
I sit in the chair, as is my custom.
With the chair turned part way out.
I watch how the light rises
along the floor,
and then along the wall.
Sometimes I close my eyes,
I sleep.
I dream.
I dream of you.
I wake.
I see the light, and the room.
And where the light does not reach.

A day of mischief.
Many reports and strange associations.
I saw you as you had been,
but older.
I put you older in your young days.
And laughed.
How silly you looked.
I did the same with myself.
I sat down deep in the chair.
I looked around.
I took the light
and dressed it in other clothes.
I laughed and laughed.

A letter,
it had my name.
It had your name.
I opened it.
I read what it said.
I read and my eyes saw.
I turned to the light
and I showed it the letter.
It is from you I said.
I told the light.
Then I returned to the letter.

You had written me.
How happy I was.
I read the words.
I looked at the words.
I saw my name
and yours.
You wrote me, and I
have the letter.

Dreams.
I have left the room.
Sometimes the chair is with me,
sometimes not.
Sometimes I feel myself rising
as if by myself.
Once I was in a park,
and I was walking.
There was a bird there.
Or was it my reflection.
It was morning, there was a park
around me.
Where the room had been
there was a park.
There was a bird.
It sang.
I woke to the bird singing.

All day I have thought of the park.
If only I could get it into the room.
If only the bird would come here
and walk.
If only the bird would stand in the light
as you had done,
crossing the light, then coming back.
If only the chair would turn
a little,
a little more,
if the bird would come, if the
light and the park would agree.
Really I think very little of the park.
I remember little.
You were not there.
Why would I want to be where you are not?

Morning. Light. The room.
Today the chair is stiff
where it once was soft.
Today the light seems old.
Did I sleep a long time?
Already it has climbed the wall.
A bit has reached the woodwork
near the chair.
Almost I could touch the light
if I could reach out,
or wanted to.

Cedar City

I am sitting here in Southwest Utah
in a classroom where my students
are taking a test
and I know now fairly assuredly—
the summer already half over—
I will not be able to write
the poems which I have wished to write.
(Last year, did it seem I could write them?)
Is it something perhaps in the water here
with which each morning
I thin the orange juice concentrate
or in the stultifying stupefying wash
of the sun—in the valley
smelted through small bits of moisture
and dust
or on the mountain above the town
frank and outright as a space heater
close to the skin?
Or is it just that I have grown tired
of poetry—that dull meditation—
here in the land of much to do?

Outside some college students
are playing a game.
It is a weird game
in which the legs of nine
persons are tied together
making a long snake
which then, curiously, as in a
three legged race, must
move sideways—the snake that is—
face first in terms of the persons
and north up the field.
And now a young boy on a skateboard
zooms past
over the pavement squares
of concrete
like a miniature locomotive.
From the south a crack of thunder
such as, for these two weeks,

has been unheard of
in this area.
And oh how well they take care
of the grass here—
each night the swoosh of
the sprinkers.

I have found it, in short,
nearly impossible to work.
Two poems are begun, but neither finished.
One about the mountains east of town—
a lake where we went fishing days ago—
but when I go into the mountains
again, last night for instance, in search
of new material,
the red rocks and the gray,
the brown volcanic rocks on which
nothing in 20 million years
has seemed to be able to take hold,
take from my lungs my breath
and from my head all hope
for words.
It is not easy to work, my friend,
in such altitudes.
To go on a poetry sortie
out from the standard brick dormitory
in which we have been housed
and go 6 thousand feet
through dangerous gorges, the
old yellow car blowing and choking,
the curves too sharp
and the grade steep as the
motel prices,
requires, for me, superhuman effort
not only of the imagination
but of the physical body as well.
Consider for one the lowly aspens—
lowly in that—they tell me—
their wood burns up like paper—is
lousy for fires—but which are
themselves splendid, and which grow
only amidst splendor, making their contribution—

which sheath themselves in a thick bark—
creamy white, the loveliest complexion—
utterly beyond the rescue or
abandonment of words.

What do I do with these great frustrations?
Do I go to my room to pout,
do I strike at my children's hopes by saying no?
Am I, as has been hinted at,
overly demanding of my students?
Am I belligerent at breakfast, sour
around the mouth like an unwashed
ash tray?

The problem in part I think—I think
too much how I am grateful
(Doesn't it seem that the best most
respected of modern poetry
is rarely the product of good will?)
that I have, once again,
too many to thank, too many
from whom the blessings, money,
daylight, a gentle teaching schedule,
time to myself, have flowed.
How to get all of their names
into a poem
whose purpose, it once seemed,
was to leave out all but the leaves' ministrations,
the flat impersonal look of the
landscape, and the cool relief
of the night breeze. The mountains
are spectacular (matching the people).
There I have said it. What even
the average camera can't know
what to do with. Last night
for instance, we zigged and
zagged, rode gravel, fished a creek
between two ranges, then, turning home,
too soon it seemed to us—
discovered we were full forty miles away.
Is there another land like this,
so rich with distance?

I do not think there can be legitimate poems
written of such a place.
I think it is its own poem.
It would surprise me very much
if in the next 30 years
a poet was born and or grew up
and wrote about Cedar City Utah
and the surrounding sumptuous mountains.
Even if he or she went away to college
took many lovers (most of whom were
properly disasters)
journeyed the far world,
and proved, beyond a doubt,
that he or she was capable of
the various challenges a poet faces—
the difficulty of making new metaphor,
"the line" and all it means
(nowadays a gradual loosening, yes
even the loss of the line as in
the recent work of that poet of
formerly such sure lines, his poems
seemed networks of carefully laid out
streets, all with high curbs—
the whole problem of imagery—
what precisely the poet can expect
the reader to have gone through—
the same bar mitzvahs, a fall down stairs,
trees along a suburban lane,
beyond which lawns ripen toward
mint julep glasses, ice clinking
around tennis courts, the houses of
rich lost sad slow days—
or vagabond images
cut lumber, cactus flowers,
a poncho set on the ground
so that a man and woman eat their stews
or might lie down, and over them
God's or the godless stars.

I do not even think (do you?) that
poetry expresses the extant—instead
it makes a new place—set in
terms of this landscape of mountains

and canyons—but a place one cannot
get to exactly—a kind of mirage
where half seeing is our full substantiation.
After all, the world is wordless. The
hummingbird I came upon today
at Cedar Breaks seemed totally
unaware either of my presence
or of the gut-sucking immensity
of the huge broken ground behind
our backs—100 miles of view—
great heaps of pink earth, and
the earth falling away. He climbed
and dived at incredible speeds—
swooping down so near the ground
I thought he would bash his little head in—
bend his bill like a too-fine needle
against dry leather—the wings
a kind of mechanical blur—
but softer—
and all for a few flowers.
We did not, of course, speak.
And in the sky above us,
what a blank yet inevitable parchment.

Any future poet Utah might produce
must reckon with these mysteries,
not with himself.
And yet, perhaps another course
might offer the lesser resistance.
One can be as sick here, as pained,
as in another place. I have heard already,
for instance, from persons who are
more or less unhappy—and even myself
written these last two weeks—
immense morasses of slime, primeval muck,
dark confessions of hope and despair.
Perhaps such bleak comedies
are a natural reaction to
having to live in a place so inexpressibly lovely,
a land the hand of man has been
unable, thus far, to bring down.

One, one might say, that's not been accommodated
to either the bucky beavers of smoke
and shine, or the crab monsters
of drab living quarters.
Even at Brian Head, thirty miles away,
the one ski area, yet to be developed,
looks like 6 bandaids
on an elephant—
and the elephant not yet aware
of the imposition.
But speaking of poetry, as we were,
is one always supposed to be happy?

To think of the poet of Cedar City Utah
this yet unborn, unreckoned, or undiscovered
genius of tree and lake
must be, at last, a momentary occupation.
I can do little more than acknowledge
my own frustration, my own reluctance
likewise to give up, to pass the baton
to the next runner (was it ever mine to pass).
How I have loved this place.
How I have loved this race
even if all uphill. Outside, as I sit here,
a group of happy people go by talking.
Matters concerning poetry do not
concern them.
Around me, within the immediate confines
of this room, pencils are squeaking shut,
the pens dry up, the brows of
the students go flat again as Kansas.
The hour it seems is over.
This other pleasant diversion draws
to a close. How tired I am—
having written only a few lines—
yet how pleased to be stepping out
into the blond daylight, preceded
by a knot of test takers.
I see from my place on the
veranda of the Music Hall
the flag of our country and

the state flag blowing strong
in the wind over the water
fountain. Strains of a virtuoso
music emanate from a study room
nearby. Someone, like ourselves,
has found this place sufficiently diverting,
and beats his pleasant practice out
while the world turns.
Now the Utah afternoon begins.
How gracefully the day assumes its middle age.
How beautiful the prospect
of an hour and a half
on the racketball courts
across the street from my local residence.

Jawbone

1

That jawbone by the tree
the dogs brought home.
That was a year ago
before life kicked the shit
out of the dogs and me.
But not before it ripped
the jawbone off
whatever it had been that wore it.
I can see
(and it is clear)
life's kicked the shit
out of many more than me
and some it did worse to.
My father for instance
had the shit kicked out of him
three times at least.
First by his wife, our holy mother,
then by me,
then by my brother's slaughter on the road.
Mother is another.
Her wretched job,
excelled in boring cruelty
only by the tedium of her soul.
What shit is left in her—
and it is a good deal—
I'm doomed to kick
starting tomorrow apparently.

2

Life and death and time
sit in a room and drink.
They do not have to think.
They idly flick their ashes on the floor.
One of them goes to the door.
Today let's kick the shit out of Sally Jones.
Hear hear, rah-rah.
And Sally Jones goes down.
Sally of the happy smile
who brought her grandma like Red Riding Hood
a pleasant afternoon in the woods of her soul.

3

My friend Bob
a water colorist
worked hard on doing bridges and twigs
ate, for his health,
brown rice, celery by the ton,
carrot juice,
would not eat figs,
potatoes or ice cream—
they were too fattening—
got the shit kicked out of him
anyway,
cancer of some blob of an organ
poor slob didn't know he had.
Died as a little fistful of pain,
buried by his dad.

4

A smile a day, a bird, a
flower in a buttonhole.
We walk the corridors of light
we put on clothes, we put on
happy smiles, we laugh.
We dance, we sing, we try to
make things right.
The seasons run us down,
storms.
The dead reach up and snare
our passing feet.
The grass rolls over us.

5

You say you are glad for the sun.
Tomorrow it will go.
You say you are holding your own.
Tomorrow they will leave.
You say you are improving, that you feel stronger again.
Forget it friend, you will collapse.
You say you have much to learn.
Oh you will be forgotten.

6

I was simply walking down the road
minding my own business, wearing a happy smile
smelling the scents of flowers, listening to the
whispers of the grass, watching the dogs
work in the bushes, two hours later
I was down on the floor in the kitchen
getting the shit kicked out of me
the three of them really working me over
one pounding me hard across the mouth
the other pummeling my gut
the other had his fist up my ass
pulling the entrails out. Oh Jesus I said
oh Jesus.

The River

Along the river many birds take up the river.
Dipping down they streak along it, reflected there—
double their numbers. The same with the leaves.
Along the river river trees reach under to refill
themselves, then to the wind unleash their vapors.
And the river rat who loves the mud, brown as the mud
he loves, runs silently out and back against
the grain of the current, or lets it take him.
Sometimes will go upsteam, meeting the sticks
coming down. You should see the river in winter.
A good much stops, a good much stays the same.
Tree bark affronts us even more, though is
the same bark, only the leaves are down. The chief
difference is the ice, gripping first the edge
of the shore, will work its way nearly across,
allowing only the barest flow along the seam,
it in itself to close. I have gone walking there
all the way across, the ice giving under me,
but the place otherwise mute. A house in the
distance makes its appearance through trees
previously profuse, now emptier, or filled with
the smoke rising from the chimney of the house.
A red dog stands in his yard and barks, and
the sound of that barking comes down the hill
to the river. The birds remain, or many of them do,
though they seem more conspicuous if not by
color, its variety, then by the marks their feet
have left in snow, one bird doing a hundred feet.
You get the feeling of a great gathering, but
then on spying some along the shore, where the
snow is light at the edge of the ice, see
how much has been done by so few. What keeps
them here, you wonder, starved yourself on just
this short walk. Or why doesn't the river back up.
In spring it is always where it had been, and
now where the shore seemed bleak, wildflowers come.
Many colors, whites and yellows, various shades
of yellow. Right up through the downed leaves
and residue of themselves the year before, they
ascend. You walk there by yourself, or we go
out together, idle, with nothing to do, or

hearing some call. When we are here and get
restless, it always seems the river is that thing
in us most present. Why else do we go. With
the trees coming to leaf. At night, in summer,
the river seems most in voice. If not so loud
as the spring rush, when the water roiled among
the roots and tore out much of the bank on,
our side, then more numerous in its sounds.
Frogs in their midnights, the dance of mosquitoes,
the churning of other bugs, and the slow roll
of the water. I have been out along it tending my
fire, night fishing or just to relax, alone, while
you were far in some other place. What a comfort
the river is at such a time, a faint breeze
and my faint breath, a tossing in its sleep to
still me, sparing me mine. Once, in the night,
two deer, startled by something, came out into
the water and then thought better. Another time
I listened while a raccoon picked a shell
to pieces, cracking it on a rock, then sucking
on it. A strange common sound like that of my
son learning to feed himself. Once we were
gone for a whole year, returning in autumn
to a cabin demolished and lived in by everything.
A week to get them all talked out, replacing
their sounds with ours, poems instead of gossip,
gossip instead of heat. The river, all this time,
had not gone one bit down, the summer rainy.
From the shed in early September we spooked an owl.

Sometimes I will travel upsteam to where, near
its starting points, the river has more to say, or
seems to, its water more white, the turns of its
banks more sudden, and the rocks prominent.
To a certain extent the river seems less here, has
less on its mind, as I suppose in an analogy our
avid talkers, the ones who do the most among us,
suggest less depth of feeling. Here the river is
more shallow. I have walked across it in many places,
though where the current is most swift I have not
ventured. Trout abound in these waters, the current
full of feed delivers it past their noses. The times
I have fished have always produced some good catches.

The river seeming not to mind, does not flow past more
swiftly or the less for having its fish depleted.
To reside like that, the way the trout does, seems
a worthy object.

Just below our cabin there's a place to swim.
We like to lie on our backs and float on slowly
down past the mill. There a big dark log comes out,
diverts the water past its end, and forms
a hollow where we tie our rafts. The trip
taking all of thirty minutes. And sometimes
we wake from our drowse to push off into the quicker
run of the water. The mill old, its windows gone.
And the wheel washed away and broken bit by bit
and scattered on the shores and burnt for firewood
or tangled in amongst briars where nothing but a dog
can reach. If we tie up there there is a place
to sleep. The sun hard on our backs and chests.
I have been sunburned two or three times,
and paddling back, all shivers and gooseflesh,
slipped down often in the cool deep holes of
the river, to ease my skin. The river is many things.

The Night of January 12, 1978

There are many beautiful things in the world
so many in fact that they compete for our attention
and so we turn inward
where it seems things are differentiated
or, injuring ourselves in a sudden fall,
we nurse the fall. Still
at odd moments, looking up suddenly
from a cup of coffee that clears the night's dreams
from our heads, the blue jay
at the feeder! At another time the tree
behind him, in wind, would call forth praises
upon itself, or the wind, invisible
except in these respective feathers,
would blur these beauties.
But this morning the air is still
and the blue jay is not afriad
so that, if we do not rise from our chair
moving across the glass, he will
go on eating. Some necessity like thirst
as is the case this morning
lies behind all such encounters.
Most of the time when we are content—
a condition highly desirable
and which our doctors try to encourage in us
even though it would mean a sharp decline
in their profits—
we do not make such observations—
indeed, it might be said,
do not see anything at all
except perhaps
the use to which things are put or might be put
as say in that most lucrative of all professions
the practical application of basic truths.
The poet, while he lives beyond such a world
at peril to his welfare, and his sanity,
still must break loose. It is
essential not to be too comfortable—
but then this is so obvious and you know
it already.

Beautiful things! I had intended to name them.
But perhaps I must leave them till later now—
this discussion having gone off into a strange
unexpected region—but that is the genius
of poetry. To call it back would—well—
restore an order destructive of the
spontaneity of art, which, though much
is made of it, and nearly all poets claim it,
is in fact a rare thing.

We were talking instead about comfort
and I can see how easily we can interpret that
in physical terms, and often it is
a measure of TV sets and money
and people over to dinner, good wines,
but this is not the fearful comfort
which can smother us, or insulate us
from the world, to such a degree, that
we are lulled as if to a real sleep.
I am talking about the need to be at odds.
Our deaths, after all, await us,
casually in the future
like so many newspapers left on porches,
like car accidents, tragic yet
compulsive (one just destroyed my previously
invulnerable-seeming brother—twenty-five years
old, who had fucked maybe only three or four
women, and not all that well probably,
who had written not one published poem—
and who, in dying, has broken not only
his mother's heart and his father's heart,
which is somehow inevitable under the
circumstances—but who has also destroyed
my life, the one I've known these past 9 years.
And I sit here my guts ripped out and
my eyes run red in sorrow).

Death, I assure you, resides in the
very fiber of existence, the louse under
the blue jay's wing, for instance, is there
for the careful viewer. Ubiquitous, its
agents, and every day, every second of every day

some celebration of its potency. We must
not, therefore, stay too even with the world,
failing thereby to see its essential
lack of hospitality—or if that seems too
harsh a judgment—the day being lovely—
and you can forget my brother's miserable death
(while I cannot)
then phrased perhaps better as a sudden
rambunctious denying of that hospitality.
The true poet knows this truth
or that is what all men know
although his knowing of it may not
be entirely conscious, and though he
may never write a poem ostensibly about
the monster, still he knows that
permanence is a lie, and it is the fading
that calls us, and against which we measure our
courage, and which will, in its final
formation, draw us away forever.

Why write under such a burden?
How is it possible? Doesn't it seem that all
joy has been cancelled, that darkness rules.
It was of course my brother's very rapture
at his happiness—he had just made some
very positive decisions—which caused him
to drive the car faster than he would have—
and encouraged his carelessness.
I admit that it is in part
curiosity, not only for seeing what
might be made of such a nightmare—
suicide being the other alternative—
but also because one clings inflexibly
to life, no matter how assailed. One can
it is said, be rescued right up
to the very last moment—there are
cases of people saved from drowning
by lifeguards who just barely reach them—
or being suddenly tossed by the surf
into water shallow enough to permit them
to come to their feet
thus allowing their escape—

of the even more miraculous escapes
for which one feels drawn to use another
vocabulary, and to talk about salvation—
where the individual, blighted by despair,
works out through some miracle,
a reasonable expectation for further life
even if it be merely to nurse his pain
into an educable creature
which will, someday,
be set free into the world
and the patient—let us call him that,
for pain of this sort
debilitates everyone—
free also.

This I can tell you
is one of my fondest hopes
indeed perhaps the only one
so do not laugh at me
if I seem clutching at straws
perhaps it is so
but would you want to be in my shoes
certainly not
and I would not want you there.

The poet, I think, can never truly
count himself a poet
until, in a like circumstance,
he is truly tested. How hard it is
to praise or to blame life
when nothing day after day occurs.
When one's diet is all that one watches
and not for the sake of prevention of disease—
but because there is little else
which is a possible variable.
Sure, everyone has bad days, and
there is sadness everywhere.
The truly tragic is always just around
the corner—
could one know the contents of
that old man's mind, which
saw the deaths of myriads of things—

oh how one could write.
I dreamed this as a boy, and
thought I saw—myself—beyond the veil.
Physical deformities, as a certain stoop
to the shoulders of the old,
of the doomed shuffle of their feet
crossing the street—
these were my images, my evidence.
Or the lack of communication
between my father and me—
though it never reached the level
of physical violence—
which now I see
could have been truly terrible
and life prohibiting—
nothing like this occurred—
yet my overly sensitive nature—
which early on I think
thought of itself as the soul of a poet
and was encouraged in that delusion
by my mother's indulgence—
took up these things and laid the doormat
of the sufferer outside
and closed the door. Ten years
I wrote like this—fifteen—
until, 4 months ago,
my brother, misjudging a bit of distance,
and maybe partially drunk—
on the wind perhaps or beer—
smashed his brains into a pulp
on a hill a mile or so
from the place he was born
a mile from the streets
where as a kid he went
along with me and shovelled snow—
and where his own dreams took shape
against the great odds of his
birth and fortune.
This stops my tongue.
This strikes a 2x4 across my writing arm—
cracking the bone.
This pours blood into my mouth

and ice down my throat.
I sit here in the chair and squirm—
there is a blade cutting me—
and no matter where I move
it lacerates.
Jeff, Jeff I call out—
but it is too late, the car
is already out in the passing lane—
the warm September dusk lends a
security to the scene—
then BANG—his car's hit,
his body is thrown violently forward
against the wheel
smashing the ribs,
the organs of the abdominal cavity
mangled by the shift lever
then the head goes forward
into the hard dashboard and glass—
face I have loved, shoulders
propelled by their own healthy weight
leading the body to its doom
arms strong, tanned from a summer's work
and play, 3 fishing trips,
helpless now,
and oh I am screaming now
God damn fuck son of a bitch
God damn God damn the
bastards into the phone.

I can talk here all I want about misery
because now I know a little of what
it means to be miserable.
Yet this is but a small part of the problem.
The hostility set loose in me
is itself a disaster, and all consuming in
its passion. I would, I can tell you,
strike down all goodness, I would,
madman that I am, become the
cripple I have always despised—
that wraith that was the angel of our family,
and infused so many moments that we
lived and tried to live.

A car is inside me like Jeff's car
going a hundred miles an hour
and business as usual
around every bend, children playing
in the streets, and some of them
mine, dogs I love lying on their backs
in the sun, and the dew just
now going up, invisible, into the sun's face.
Oh how I hate myself.
Oh how I hate what I have been
and dreamed to be.
My company I find loathsome.
My breath stinks.
My poems, my thoughts are ugly,
encrusted with waste and disease.
Still, the world is lovely beyond me.

I meant to speak of those things
and indeed I will.
Resident within me, remaining,
are those aspirations at least
of a good man. I have, it can be said,
a sufficient memory, and I
do not throw over without an argument
a vision of life which was essentially benign,
optimistic, and which cherished loveliness.
I do remark, for instance,
the snow. It is not much,
but it covers the ground, makes the
ground white, concealing the dry earth,
and the leaves most of them down now.
And that it has been cold enough
lately to retain the snow—
and even, tonight, the forces so
favorably in conjunction,
to frost the windshield of the car
making pretty patterns.
As well my son and daughter thrive.
To them nothing has happened.
To them it is Thursday or Monday
a night of TV
or Daddy will make homemade soup

or tonight we will go out to eat Yippee!
And my wife too
is part of what is good.
How she goes on, watching me as I
collapse, struggling in the ways she knows.

Each of us is trained for just a few things.
It may seem sometimes that we are
insufficient,
but often the circumstances are beyond us.
No one can defeat all terrors.
Each must go down at the end
under his own unbearable pain.
We would like to have it elsewise
but this I think is how it is in the world.

A Person in My Life

My father ascends
and now he comes down.
My father is eating his breakfast
in peace and quiet
and then he goes out to the yard.
The yard has grown small around him.
My father is sleeping, now he awakes,
my father has dreamt of himself as a child.
My father has seen his brother gone off
to the war, his sister insist on the money.
My father is lonely, worse than before.
My father has gone to the woods
where the snow is deep.
All night it has risen against the trees.
He walks in the snow there
carrying me.
My father is glad that the dream is of snow.

Into the attic he goes, hand over hand.
Into the darkness of books
with the pages missing, books
in another language.
In the old high school yearbook
he looks for himself, for his face,
as once long ago as a boy I looked for my father.
As once in the future my son and my daughter
will come to imagine me.
He tries on all the old clothes,
he tries on all the old dreams.
And none of them fit.
He has grown and diminished in odd ways.
He has left them for decades in boxes,
in darkness, and now
when they're called on
not one will come.
Not one will slip over head and arms.
Not one will marry the present and past.
My father assumed it would happen.
My father had guessed he would lose.
My father decided and so it is so.

When I went to find you father
a long time ago
I found the glasses and the cups
you washed
stacked on the rubber mat
next to the sink
and I asked them
where you were
how they had let you get away.
They said the door might know
so I went to the basement door
down the stairs you walked
a thousand times
but I did not meet you
coming up.
I asked the stairs why they
did not hold you in your shoes
I asked the workbench
which still held your tools
what you looked like to them
to tell what they knew
that whole bench full
but not one spoke
not one hammer, not one blade or screw.
How loyal they are to you.
Not even the dust under the bench
would tell.

In a rented boat one day
with the sun a breeze upon us
we set out from the hard packed beach
over the lily padded water
over the blue lagoon
to fish. You driving,
me in the bow catching the wind head on,
watching the water slide under the boat,
and hearing the motor as if far off,
as with one arm you leaned back to it,
your face somewhere back there in the sky,
holding it like you would a woman.
I remember the day in the fall
you showed me to walk on tiptoe

through the steep ravine
with the gun cradled, shells in my pockets,
looking for grouse,
and finding instead
only the weather.
I remember us coming to rest
in a grove of trees
the coffee hot in the tin cup.
I remember the night you came home
from the clambake
drunk and the coins in your hand
to show us you'd not lost
all your money,
dropping them one at a time
into mother's reluctant palm.

It is late as you stay awake
in the old house
from which we have all set forth into the world
except yourself.
Keeper of the past
maker of half my dreams.
The streets you brought me up on
have grown furious with cars.
The neighborhood's infected by another time.
The once sheltering lilacs have grown past
their spread and now,
as slender poles, crack-barked,
they lean and bake or freeze
and will not keep your privacy.
In spring they're nearly leafless
with just a few flowers.
The dog's dead. Mom's left.
And no one calls you on the telephone.

You told me men grow sad.
If they are lucky they are old.
You told me men grow weak and tire
in spite of everything.
If they are lucky they are dead.
The world's wrong, a great no place,
no singing, no pets, no dreams.

With such an outlook
I was fitted.
It came down over my face
like veil or helmet.
I walked around for years
in those gray clothes.
I built it up, day into dusk,
light into night.
Grew sad as you grew old.
Grew up as the gray stone rose.

I remember that kitchen
its waxed panels of pine.
The cupboards you built endlessly
month after month
in the cellar, then
with my help lugged up the narrow
stairway, sparing them bruises,
fitting them tight to the walls,
bolting them down. On Saturdays,
a month of Sundays, you worked,
finding the dream. The floor
already laid down carefully,
the old linoleum whisked away,
that ugly dark blue rubbed and scratched,
in big sheets peeled,
replaced by little squares
of veined gray. The sink
you bought new, but not the
stainless steel, the porcelain again,
for it was weight you loved,
preferring always the heavy
over the lighter thing—built better
if it could not be lifted,
best if it never moved.
Things you installed yourself were best.
Now eighteen years beyond those days
the kitchen doors swing tight
on hard hinges, and the sink
holds water. Only the dishes
are new, new purchased when my
mother took the old.
Everything you laid your hand to
built to last except her love.

Rubbed by the world in one right way
like wood I achieved a fine finish.
My teachers dumped the polish on
and elbow greased me clean.
Far from your house I weaned,
took on my wax, and shone.
Far from the workbench dungeon
of your self
I learned another lore.
I strove, my body like a prized loaf
buttered with a fine shellac.
Yanked from their ovens
they pronounced me done.
Brought to your table,
almost you took me back.

I see a great room
where we meet
and you are in charge.
I see how the guns are laid out
so carefully
each waxed in its oil, and glittering.
Today we will shoot each other
across the dining room table.
Today we will assemble the heavy revolvers
and load them,
and then we will sit down to eat.
We will talk and the talk will turn bad.
We will sit there and fume
as the sun goes down into snowbanks.
Mother will serve up the cupcakes in tears,
my brother will drop to the floor
on all fours,
the dog crawl out to the hallway.
Then we will shoot point blank
into each other's words.

When you came to find me father
I was less than you,
a mere vibration set in motion by your voice.
When you bid me hold the board end
where you worked

my mind went off like birds
into the dusk.
I had no hands, no posture for that job.
Pinched by a feeling I could not bear,
distracted always by myself,
foot clumsy, impetuous,
my life with you
was one long huge abstraction.
Failing, I did not hit
the nail on the head,
failing, I did not drop the log
at the proper moment.
What work I did I did alone
you came behind to finish
doubling your time.
Taking the life from mine.

A gray sky, snow deep in the driveway,
the sound of your shovel scraping the gravel
as I lie high in the room, warm
in the covers.

Not once did I help you shovel out.

That road you traveled, 15 miles,
I've learned my own way now.
It is plain, where you go,
as is my own. A few houses,
some cows in a field,
and the trees come down to the road
or held back by fences.
A left turn and a right, like mine.
And the sound of the motor
vaguely threatening,
and under us the road unsure in its ice.

I am through hating you.

The Dream

I went to the house of the dead last night
in my dream
and there was my brother
fresh killed
balanced as if to run on the balls of his feet
wearing the shock of his death
like a shirt too large
like a shirt which had suddenly shrunk
up beyond his wrist bones
in the wash
like the sweater that would not shrink
his girlfriend Marsha made
with sleeves come down two inches past his fingers
which all one day we washed
and stretched upon the kitchen table
hung in the dark to dry
my brother—
loved best of all my family—
stuck in his own still certain corner
face to the steering wheel
mind sorting over and over again
the day's few solitary hopes

as he had been in life
always
as I remember
off to elsewhere
always poised on the balls of his feet
standing up a little higher on the toes
like a dog stretching to have his back scratched
getting ready always to leave
packing to leave, waiting,
sitting, smoking in a chair,
for out of the rain
his ride, his friend, his friends, dream,
lover
to arrive.
He was as I had seen him last
in life, the same uncertain man,
the same man quick to anger and regret

the same pack of Camels stuck
in his blue jean jacket pocket, the same
—on his fingers—stains.

Last night I went in my dream
to the house of the dead
and there was my brother freshly dead
with all about the same air, the same look,
the same black curly hair, and the face skin
coarse with the irrepressible beard
the same long fingers, tough nails,
the same tough calloused finger tips
earned from long years at the guitar
the frustration of guitar and tools
and the same in the eye look
of trapped hurt, look of sadness,
look of lost things, dead ends,
hope.

And they were all there with him.
All the dead of ours, all the new dead
and the old, sitting or standing about
as I remembered them,
as memory keeps them still—from
daylight into dream and out again—
my grandma, old Estelle, who died
a year before my brother
sitting as she always did, in a chair
too big for her, with nothing in her hands,
and her face blank but kind
and the flesh pale white
hung down below her arms, the flab
I played with as a child, when she
lived in our house and mothered me.

And Jeff was there beside her in the same
stiff silence which prevailed in life.
And it was just the same between them
as it had been, nothing
to say, no kind look, no touch, no arm
put over a shoulder, no hand in hand

for the hurts there, for the common blood
that kept both bodies warm.
It was just as it had been in life,
the two unspeaking, and nothing to say.

I went to the house of the dead last night
in my dream
and stood among the dead
and heard them breathe
and watched them go in separate globes of light
among their things, and sit, and
rise from bed,
and fall back down again.
My grandma with her lampshades and her bathing caps,
all day to make, the little stitchings
on the throwaways, that no one saw or loved,
my brother Jeff cranking the motor to a scream
and blazing off into the great
inexhaustible mile.
And they were not alone.
And mother also there (will she die soon?)
my father too, who lives in liquor and regret
(will he die soon
because I saw him there?)
All, there, in the great house of the dead
my mother over her pot roast
the table set, the plastic flowers, the
gleaming pots and lids, the copper brought
out bright, the napkins pressed and firm, the
dishes scrubbed, over her stew, her casserole
and there, beside her in the dark,
the dark of self, a self of otherness,
was Jeff awaiting the dinner he didn't want,
as fifty-hundred times
he stood, and bit his nails, and smoked,
while the stew pot cooked.

My father too in the house of the dead, dark,
somber, a face where no smile lived, where
no laugh ever bloomed, or poked
even a green bud through,
as in life, as he had been, as he is
in life,

there in the gloom of the dead house
come in just then
the big back door
clutching the black lunch box
with the sour smell of milk
come to the room of ripening bananas in a dish
opening the more ripe box
to let the peel smell out
the sour-mouthed thermos
letting in just for a moment
the flash of day before
the big door closed.
And I a little boy run in to see it close.
As he had been, as we had been, in life.

Last night I went to the house of the dead
in my dream
and saw how the living died
and what they did,
and saw how the dead live.
Saw that it was the same,
that it was all the same as it had been
in life, how the stew pot cooked
and the lunch box lay on the counter top
in the darkened room
and there, on the balls of his feet
poised to escape,
my brother stood and stood and stood,
and did not move, and did not
get away.

This morning the sun came in the window
and I woke.
I turned in the big bed of my own life,
in the living world,
and let my legs stretch down along the bed,
to the cool spot at the bottom of the bed,
and rolled my arms about,
and turned, and felt
the warm place where my wife had slept
and from which minutes earlier she'd left
and gone out
out from the room.

And taken off to school the children
and herself.
I heard the car begin, rumble, go,
I heard it swish the driveway hedge, and go,
or just another car
blowing the leaves along the street,
and felt still in the terror of the dream,
and felt still in me
fear for my own life,
felt in the bed my mortal form,
felt the heat go out of the place
my wife had slept,
into the cool big air of the room,
feared for her flesh gone off in the car,
for the flesh we came together to make,
for the hole in the world
inside which each man lives, each woman,
for globes of light in darkness,
for all the children, our children,
the children who are ourselves,
for all the living dead,
for all the dead
still living in our minds,
for all the living soon to die,
and broke down to a sweat,
and laughed, and bent as if in birth
or pain,
and cried out.

Songs

The mudlark sings its sad song.
So too the Spanish cormorant.
And I have heard the Garth flamingo
burleying at midnight, far from home.
Did you regard the lost last cry
of Thomas Arthur's Bulfinch mewing?
These are all sad singers, singers
of sad dark songs, beautiful in their way,
despite the mood, the overriding underscoring
heaviness, the negative aspects,
the lack, it may be argued,
of a sufficient balance. What rights
have they, I should like to ask myself,
these whose province is sunlight and
water (which is another light) (or
a light twice) to be acting so deprived?

Monday:
the curlews are twittering. Breakfast
at nine thirty. Awakened earlier, sevenish,
by the musketry of the hen hawkers,
an Audubon dishevelment. Trees
were flush in leaves, with wind.
Around ten, after forcing down some sopped toast,
blew out myself into the yard.
Called by the cardinal's entreaties,
attracted by the robin and her red cry.
A big mayhawk was perched like a piece of iron
or meteor, like a pinnacle on the garage,
its shadow drooping like wet raincoats
over the gravel.

Oh they are all lovely these singers.
They are all forgettably present, their
colors fading, their feathers fly about and
fall, fall out, go back to dust, and yet
these songs, their songs, deep as worry,
stay as a river through me.
Below the ear, down where the bones start.

Henry calls. A big trip into blue tip country.
Lots of provisions, set out on the back of
the crosscountry van. Emergency rations,
glasses, and recording books, reams, reels,
and the table of species. Jake will join us
at midpoint, a little high hill town,
poor on water and culture, thick with scenery.
"The Blue Tip ventures a wide radius from its
nest, deposits home three dark brown eggs,
blue tipped, from which derives the name.
The call, pure poetry."

In a clearing of stones we have made our fire.
In a thicket of thick trees we have placed our
stacks, sticks, jets and bricks, bats and racks.
The younger man is wild and green, he snorts
about decapitating ferns. And then from somewhere
overhead and to our right, knick knocking
through the trees, the Blue Tip sends her
luscious notes for free.

Back. The yellow newspapers.
Mail swollen in the mail slot. One piece—
a catalog from J and Edward's Sanctuary Press,
a big swollen picture of the Alder Hawk, feet
tucked sharply into a small rodent, looking
forlorn, the wash above them both an incipient
yellow. Sally writes. Bill. Charles
is up the peninsula, deep in. Last heard
from (like a Mirabelle Warbler really when he
gets excited) had reached the Far North Roosting
Place, intact, all the slides clear, the
tapes spinning. The lawn had come up
nearly to my boottops but I walked around.
Out by the tin shed, under the martin houses,
a shrivelled gray piece like a Brodkin's Tweeter
lay in the grass and sun. I examined the beak,
the little nasal grooves. And then, from the south,
and crossing, the shadow of the Grosshawk
past the fence, disintegrating at my feet.
A hunger welled up in me, and thirst.
The silence of being fully present,

an ache along the forearm, being fully home.
And let the fragment fall, flightless,
and went back in.

Morning

1

This morning the yard tingles with light.
The special trees, straining at their roots
in self consciousness,
remind me of myself uprooted, adrift over the world.

This morning the yard holds the light in its palm.
I feel that there are many things
I have grown beyond,
but this place is not one of them.
Water is lying in the lip of the driveway gutter,
and all the lawn about me is freshly wet.
Fuck the world, I say,
the liars and killers reach even here.

This morning the yard is lying open to the sun
and wind
but the clouds make a film in the sky
and little light falls.
The dogs are in their pen
poking their faces out of the doorway to their house.
I have left my own house
wearing a blue coat and long face
mourning the dead.

2

I walk around in and amongst the bushes.
You would too.
Here are the peonies
whose blooms are ruins, dry and feathery.
Here are the poppies
grotesque on their long stalks,
only the seed head left,
not even sexual.
And there is the place
the bush with no name stood
all last year and the one before
and earlier
until it had grown to immense size
then died.
There the stump sits, the many stumps.
And around them the new shoots rising.

3
This morning I am adrift over the waters of the earth.
I want nothing, no one to talk to,
no one to sit beside on the step.
This morning I hear the birds
but they are not necessary to me.
Motion is everything, then stopping.
Feeling the damp concrete under me,
feeling the toes of my shoes grow cold in the tall grass.

Moonlight

The moonlight stews in the yard.
The yard stews in moonlight.
The yard is steeped in moonlight. There
is moonlight on the plants like lacquer
The moonlight seems present over the things
in the yard like cloth. The plants,
the trees and bushes, seem one sidedly leaning
or reaching into the moonlight.
Above the yard the moon sits, stands, is.
Then there is a large area of sky that is black
except there seems to be light in it.
Where there are clouds the clouds are very white
and seem to hold the moon within them.
Something similar is happening in the yard.
Something similar and yet different.
I was tempted to say very different,
but I am not sure I can support any assertion.
One thing I know for sure is that the moon
has come into the yard, or rather
its light has fallen upon the things of the yard.
The moon has come into the yard or over it,
has made its presence felt in the yard.
The night is very bright.
It is because of the moon.
The darkness in the yard lies always out of reach
of the moonlight.
These dark regions seem especially dark now,
but one must be sure to offer that with the
pervasive moonlight the darker areas are smaller
and a good deal less scary.
It is fun to be in the yard on such a night.
For minutes I stand out in the moonlight
waiting for it to cease.
It does not cease.
There is going to be much moonlight in the yard
tonight.
I do not know whether to stay or go,
and then upon leaving, going into the house,
a strange feeling overcomes me.

There is a sense of motion, the bottom dropping out
somewhere, the sound of rushing water.
A restlessness comes over me,
and I rush breathlessly out into the yard.
The whole yard is infused, full up, bathed
in moonlight.
It falls upon my hands and my bare arms.
It glistens there.
Presumably it also falls upon my face.
I stare all around, both upwards and on the horizontal,
trying to take it all in.
What an amazing night this is!

Maybe

Maybe the love his father lost in looking for another love
got spent and in some darker place returned upon
frail things its real disdain.
Maybe that his mother had not loved, or loved too well
some small wrong thing, and, needing it so much
to come on back to her, her self to hold her self,
the thing returned, which did not come, the world deaf
to that, in a corner of her heart she made a corner
with a house.
Maybe it was the wrong season, the autumn indecision
upon them, coming upon them too soon because some greater
    season,
national disgrace, a furor, a terror of war,
the loss of dignity staring into blank shop windows,
maybe it was this.
Maybe it was bitterness up in the throat, of not
having clothes that fit, of not being told yes
even once in a while, of not having your full name
remembered, of the phone hanging limp on the wall.
Maybe these contributed.
Or maybe it was the essential madness in the match.
The woman quick and glaring like a butterfly, or
a bee, the man heavy and deep, lead, grease under the nails,
or maybe it was some incident between them
accentuating some small difference into some nightmarish
impasse, some Matterhorn made from the fact he did not
wear a shirt to the table, showing his hairy chest.
Or that he was partly deaf that the whole world seemed
hard of hearing. It did not hear them, either laughs
or later when they cried, each in his own way.
Maybe it was her looking for a father to be father to her
    loneliness
and he, not for a mother, having had so much a mother,
but looking for a father too, and both of them
hard at his throat, watching him rise, asking
is this a man, is this a man enough.
Maybe it was the loneliness in this wind, the color
of the house, the condition of the shingles, so worn they were
when they moved in, the work all left from person to person
and now left to them.
Maybe it was not the work but the silences around the work,

the gathering places, the places of supposed storage and
rejuvenation.
Lacking these, lacking enough of them, lacking a sufficiency
of these, the work became too much, the work became
everything, and they become two midgets to the work.
Maybe it was the succession of small abatements, of
little wearings out, his watch, the transmission on the car,
the belt to her dress. Maybe it was her mother
who lived with them, bringing with her all her own
lack of fulfillment, her habits skin deep but throwing light,
her smoking.
Maybe it was her mother's smoking
which so aroused the husband's smoking,
or that caused him to take up smoking.
Or maybe it was the presence in the house of so much smoke,
the three of them all smoking
and the attendant rush for ashtrays, for compassionate sharing.
Or the day was too long.
Or in the windows of those many years she saw X and he
   saw Y.
Or maybe when he stepped out into the water of the
   trout stream
the fishing line he bought because it was cheap
snapped in trying to bring in the huge trout,
the one he could have been proud of,
the one they would all have believed,
thus speaking, here is a man, here is a man's fish.
But failed to land on account of the cheapness
of the fishing line,
on account of the stars in her eyes on seeing the dress
in the window, on account of the beer he had to purchase
on account of the presence of the mother there,
or of the absence in the woman of the father,
the beer to drench the sore place that the truth found
over and over, the place the flies went towards
smelling the irritation.
Maybe it was the two cultures bouncing off each other,
the west and the east, the dream of more
against the dream of less, or the dream of getting back
against the dream of finding first.
Maybe it was the children, or the first child,
coming out of her, of sex leading to that, or the
penis throb, cunt throb, leading to that, to shit smell,

to cries in the night, to the anguish of confusion,
the dismay of innocence amidst experts.
Maybe it was a hard ironic face at the edge of a bill,
a white building with a waiting room,
a sore throat or, in the middle of the night,
a fever that would not come down,
an agony shifting from one to the other,
and a fever running up and down wracked limbs.
And a bill at the end of it they could not pay.
Maybe it was a girl in a red dress with hair thrown
free to the wind, saying take me wind, I offer no resistance,
I have no mother no father hole no dream, no brother ache,
no missing limb, no back dying to bend under some immensity.
And breasts that winked and scoffed and loafed inside
her shirt.
Maybe it was a smooth cheek on a man, a white bright shirt
on a man who stood in the light and laughed and heard
the world and sold for cash
something clever and necessary,
and did not get wet or tired or hurt.
Maybe dreams overtook them.
Maybe the dreams of something elsewhere, wanting to
     go elsewhere,
or going together going at different speeds.
Maybe it was speed they differed over,
how fast to bring it about, this improvement, this
step in the right direction.
Maybe they were in total agreement but they differed over
the pace of the operation, or maybe it was not the speed
but the tone.
Maybe it was the tone, one wanting to be firm and resolute,
the other not seeing, or the old one thinking it was slipping,
seeing the other casual to it, not noticing,
or maybe the one who aged first stopped and then the other
slipped past, speeding forward into its arm, getting fat
getting gray, getting tired, the sentences failing to
complete themselves, failing to be tough and clear.
Maybe it was how he snored all night, shaking the room,
or the way he left beside the bed his underpants.
Maybe it was she, maybe it was how she hung on the
     bathroom rod
her scrubbed out underpants, this hurting him,

this distracting him from his wrench and pliers.
Maybe it was something else.
Maybe it was when they met, he seeing something on the
     way out
of her, she seeing something in him that was fading,
something another woman had called up and then abandoned,
he trying to wipe it off his face, she trying to rid from herself
this thing another man had asked her to become,
but which she could not become,
but which she had tried to become.
Maybe that was it,
Maybe the meeting was wrong, the first time seeing
each other.
Maybe if each had said what will this lead us to,
or even if one had said, do we know what we are seeing,
or even after they were going together for a time,
even after they had kissed and laughed
and gone places, even after the first disagreement,
and all that wonderful room for reconsideration between
the first and the second disagreements,
maybe there, or in the further space after the shirt was off,
the breasts in the other light of afterwards,
or when the breath stank from cheese or beer,
or when the nose ran,
or when from out of the body there came the stench
of corruption, or
from out of the mind some immense triviality,
some proof that in the midst of him, or her, a mad map
ruled the going, a chart of a different plague was in him,
a foreign language lay beneath each word, or
half a word.
Maybe it was not early but later.
Maybe the early was good.
Maybe in comparison to what they had each known
this other stranger beckoned sweet and the light shone.
Maybe they could have done no better, each
being all that he was, all that he wanted to stretch from,
all that birth and fate and place and color of hair
and eye and height and weight, these presences,
declared.
Maybe they did not try enough.
Maybe seeing it going, even when it was good, how it
slipped a bit and went, flying, away,

maybe they should have sat and held and firmed against it,
or looked in some cellar or attic
not in the heady midst of it but at the edge, some crack
or wear or invasion, some sign of danger.
Maybe it was not that.
Maybe it was something they did do.
Maybe it was not what they knew they had avoided but
something they did together and then saw, and looking
grew averse to.
Maybe they saw in the other themselves.
Maybe in projecting upon the other themselves they were
able to detach themselves and thus witness themselves,
and came to hate themselves.
Maybe one day someone said to her
that's a nice house you have.
Maybe he was driving home one night
and in the road a deer was bleeding to death.
Maybe she would not have stopped.
Maybe he did not stop.
Maybe he is forever going back to that place.
And the snow swirling around them both.

Letter to My Brother

1

Dear Jeff Now you are dead
Big deal
You loved speed
Big deal
So now you are dead in a car
and I wake up

I wake up in my house
12 rooms
big deal
and lots of land
the dogs outside
yawn on the lawn

I touch a flower
brimful of rain and dew
it tips
a joy sets off through me
like a man running with a letter
the letter says
Jeff Kuzma is dead
who went fast
and wrecked

Dear Jeff now you are dead
and the cereal sits in my bowl
and gets soggy
I can't eat it
my throat aches
my sobs have drenched the table top

Dear Jeff
you were a big deal
you were a loved man
you went slow
I did not care
it was no big deal
what you did right or wrong
I loved you
fast or slow

morning, I wake up
evening, I sit in my chair
my feet ache my teeth ache
bad air lies in my lungs
I butt out
,another cigarette
big deal
in the fucking ashtray
Jeff
don't die don't go yet
don't slip off that ladder
heading skyward don't
be gone
seemingly forever

2

so now you are dead
the dogs yawn
the flowers tip into spring
the second since your death
a thousand cars have spun off roads
and crashed
they are carrying the bodies now
mothers lean back in horror
fathers become living waterfalls
little children look up dazed
at the whole roof falling
the long caravan
the endless leaving
running through a million homes
and Sunday the graves
and handkerchiefs

3

you were an asshole
hot for yourself big on booze
gales of laughter
something gnawed at you
you had a bug up your ass
you had a hair itching
a place you could never scratch

I would take you now were you alive with me
into my arms and break you black and blue
bite your face
smashing everything
would walk with you into my house at night
and say look at that pile of shit
sitting at the table
the brother you left
chewing his fucking nails down
winking at light
his head forever spinning nodding
the feet shuffling
the eyes red

4

Summer.
You are dead two years.
The flowers tip and open.
The grass swarms skyward.
I hear, from my chair in the sun,
the children on the street go whoosh
and splash, the pool a block away.
I hear the laundry flapping on the line,
the birds shaking the air out of their wings.
At night, sitting outside with the lap robe on,
I hear the darkness insinuating upwards
along bark and stem,
watch how the sidewalk goes away
closer and closer into the night.
All this was yours.
All this sea of loveliness warm at my elbows,
in which I swim,
in which I bathe and go,
and am condemned to.

5

You who were careless and wrong
who loved wreckage and despair
I will love you in all the fury I can give
but I will hold to myself some saving thing
some tender thing I will not kill.

The River Kleeg

Q. Why?

A. Because we were young
and the water boiled up
over the rocks
and there was a grassy spot
to take a girl
or eat a bologna sandwich
hard boiled egg.

Q. And you were happy?

A. Happy. Well we were involved.
The hands reached out
the branch was there
the sky was blue
we lived in a cool breeze
of the inevitable.
"Gift" was the shouting
of each bird.

Q. What happened? Describe a trip.

A. Typically there were two of us.
My brother and I.
He did what I could not.
I did the rest.
He made the eggs.
I cut the wood.
He rowed the boat.
I caught the fish.
But we both laughed.

Q. And you were not touched?

Everywhere we went
was our address.
I slept not one bad night
with even the rocks under me
with even the snows, the rain.
It seemed we were the children
of the snow, the rain.

If what you mean by touch
is were we hurt
I tell you there was once
I stopped to get my breath
on a long climb up a hill
Jeff knew.
I reached out for that breath
and it was there.

Q. It seems then things were good?

A. The grim catastrophe tomorrow would become
had not yet turned its headlines
in my heart.
I said, if only to the wind,
I am alive!
And pitied everyone not in my shoes.
My brother—who knows what he lived.
But I was safe.

Q. What was the river like, the River Kleeg?

A. There was a turbulence in spots.
There were big rocks, and
pools behind that looked like maple syrup.
One night a hatch of flics
came off the flats.
I lit a cigarette
beside a tree,
pissed on some lichens
near the trail
watching the steam rise.
Among the overhang of branches
near the stream
we built the fire
nestled in among the stones.
It snapped in the night air
from the sapped wood
we fed it.
Oh it talked, we let it.
We let it do all the talking.

Q. Do you think, if I could get time off
   in the spring, you could take me there.

A. It would be good to go there once again.
   But oh, dear friend, the way is lost.

A Dying

I was said no to.
Because of the face perhaps,
because the face was old,
or blue, too blue
for the table top, for the kleenex
I dabbed in an eye.
Because of the sun come glinting,
the rain walked through,
and the things seen.
I had sat waiting all morning
in darkness,
the others rising and going.
Remember when it happened
to *your* father?
Oh I expected it, to be touched,
to feel a tingle.
Enough occasions had informed me
early, they can die
right out of your sight,
a corner turned, a room laid open.
I buried my father, my mother
both in their crinkly skins.
They had been defeated
around the same time, in life,
similar conditions. His on a Tuesday,
hers mid-week as well,
and both inglorious. Then
the wash of years. I was not
done aching I don't think from his
or even up to it, did not feel it
something known, when bango
there she was, flat on her back,
and something putting the screws
to her. You could say then
I was briefed. So it did not
surprise me so
when the leaves turned rags,
when autumn broke and ran.
There are as many sorts of torture
as there are dreams. Mine,
in particular, being varied,

I was vulnerable on all counts.
To return to that knowing—a man
said nothing doing. I don't mean
a man, a man at a desk, I mean
I drew conclusions, I had read
the weather, seen the caterpillar
fluffed and thick. Younger, I had
dreamed disease, and read,
I think, a hundred books.
So when I was given directions
I took them all seriously: if I were
to walk I should walk slowly. Stairs
were nearly out of the question.
Foods I should eat seemed minor,
those to be avoided numerous,
explosively lovely. And there was that
first doctor in it who gave me some pills,
in which, he said, it would befit me
to believe. I did. I carried them
about, they jiggled in my pocket
like candies, and half the time
the kids wanted to inspect them, see
what I hid for them. No color though,
no animal shape, no sugar (none of that
please), and a texture like sandpaper.
This thing must be good for something—
popping it down. There is, he says,
a momentary lift, the elbow,
all the distant places. I felt
like dancing at midnight, one night,
then another time without them
to rise from a book I needed Hercules.
It's easy not to like him, the doctor,
who calls the shots, whose smile
comes easy for the swollen gums
as for the dying gut. But
I would not know what he knows.
Once, when considering medical school,
it was the pickled bodies
put me off. How much more fierce
the living ones, their mauves and reds,

pigskin pink, their stinks
and running spots. Looked down my throat
once and forgot, although I think
that view came back, engulfed me in
a dream. But I awoke. And in that
steady state of waking I meant to live.
As well beyond those days as possible.

Can I recall when first I noticed the
change? I would like to say
yes, that it was more or less immediate,
or that as in some horror tale,
a momentary glimpse, a curtain parted,
fur hanging out from the forced sleeve.
Or in the novel Moby Dick, the stillness
just before the beast breaks surface,
carrying all before it in relief.
But no, a ruddyness of cheek which
had been standard, gradually dispersed,
the texture of that color changed
so slightly, if at all. I noticed
once, however, going abroad, how
the cold clung, held more deeply,
how the sun seemed further—my opinion
if I had one I remember thinking
it a product of the winter.
I did go have my eyes checked,
but in the searcher's face no puzzled
look, surprise, or sympathy. He
raised me to a higher power in the
left, was all, keeping the right the same.
Or how much time passed in this
interval. As with the sun there came
a day, and not a winter one,
where the town got farther down
the road. I set out briskly
at my early rise,
(silly to do this much with a small
thing) for apples for which I was
suddenly hungry. A cool day, though
not snowing, and went down the hill
past the old places, waving first to
Elva at her line, clothes flapping,

then to Ken as he came up,
in a new car, the blue one he still
has, over the bridge, all the usual
way. But as I went I seemed to fall
away, diminish. I thought for a
minute or so the road was ice, it
seemed so slippery, the trees blowing
in wind, they seemed so skittish.
But no, the wind was down, the day
still and the road clear but for a
few leaves shining back, smooth as ice,
to which I reasoned my poor feet
could not be sensitive. Coming back
was awful. The added weight
of the apples, though so slight,
the greater ascents necessary—whatever.
When I reached the door it seemed
the whole earth plotted. I wanted
most to turn and face them all,
my pursuers, but instead undid
the latch and entered.

It seemed dark inside, darker than
it had been. Today, in that partial
light, I live. I peer deep down
into the well of books, seeing, at
best, mostly my own face, my thoughts
swirl there. This death
is for the old, who have them,
rich collections, recollections. I
have, in a box still, many of my
first poems and stories, the former
puddles and the latter merely fights.
I keep them around to remind me
of all that I've got over. Though
there is, indeed, something fresh
in the ways I couldn't say the thing
I wanted to. A girl's face, a man's
brown arm, bigly muscled, appear.
But not in the words. The day the
eyes went, wobbled in my head,
I was terribly busy, and kept at it,

typing madly, right through lunch, the
afternoon, grayer than most, stopping
at last like a runner suddenly checked
by the side ache which he'd carried
like a knife the last three miles,
unknowingly. I fell forward as if
struck from behind, my head falling
among the letters of the keyboard. A
joke, later, was how, when I hit,
the garble I made of the keys rushing
outward, struck in the air only,
the metal sticking to metal, the paper
beneath them bare. It was, I think,
my finest work.

They did not know right away what
was wrong. Tests when I awoke, an
interview, nurses around the bed,
and in my chest the sudden desire
to flee. I laughed a lot. My first
meal monstrous, shrivelled peas, a laminated
lump of meat, a jellied gravy, coffee
bitterer than dust. They thought it
was stomach trouble, they came in once
more jubilant than I had seen them,
pronouncing the illness noxious fumes
which they had traced to valves not
properly connected. One brought a
pack of X rays like a manuscript and
we sat down together, noting the rhyme
and rigor of the bone, the careful
notching where the strings were tied,
and the organs' accomodations. You are
not roomy enough he said. Or on another
day, a lightweight intern, finger in
book, showed me a word I could not read,
which meant my eyes were but a side effect.
They searched for a name, as if
I did not matter but as audience. As
audience I cheered them to go on,
enjoying the box seat, the ringside.
And then they tired of my little jokes,

my inexplicables, my mute condition,
and they went. I followed, luckily,
a few weeks later.
You'll hear it now, what you've been
waiting for, the sweet and sour song
of the retiree. I didn't like the heat.
Palm trees made me itchy. I didn't like
and do not like the following: sand,
gravel, palm trees nestled there,
broad avenues with shallow puddles
marking, in the morning, the brief
rains. I do not like: beach people,
with their demarcations, new bathing
suits, the swellings from squeezings,
nor plastic lawn chairs, iced tea
in frosted glasses, terry cloth or
the supposedly curative effects of
fresh air, expensively got up with the
accents of a salt breeze. Yet I
survived it, came back, stood
in the hallway one fine day, and
gloated. Heavy coated—I was
freezing—but in the pleasure of
that recent escape, renewed a bit
for all of it.

Through all this my death maneuvers me.
First, I was to be surprised.
A tug within me pushed and pushed
but scarcely could I move. I felt
ice where there had been words,
I sensed heat in my palms, like that
of small stones which had laid all
day in the driveway, and, for no
reason again, the sweat would bead out
on my forehead, a curious taste,
copper or worse, in my mouth on waking.
On waking as well I found one morning
my arm would not respond, but lay
like someone else's off beyond the
pillow, the same strange distancing
the sun had worn, the town acquired.

My meals grew briefer, the enjoyment
less, my feet under the table
blocks of wood, dead animals.
When I rise at last and move around
the kitchen, it is as if I ride
on a gigantic horse, a great stumbling
beast, upon whose back I am a slipping
saddle. Not that I knock into things,
exactly, but that they cringe from me.
I need to pick up everything twice,
swirl in the sink with the rag
again and again around the inside
of the cup to clean it.
When I pour water for tea
it is over the brink of the cup
and running down the sides in
skirmishes yet can I not stop
pouring. In the chair to read,
I am pushed off gently onto the slow
swell of the sea. The room around me
steady, but the whole house lifted
by water. The book bobs up and down
beyond my puny fingers, and a
great heat rises out of my gut.

I go in for treatment three times
a week. They are trying everything.
We meet in a large room with a
big waxed table. I sit at one end
and speak. Half of them watch me,
the others write. Later, in a room
of blue light, they poke and turn me,
bringing the great lenses close,
moving the shining plates and angles.
Hours it seems they leave me as
the wind dies, the cold comes up
through the smooth white plate, my
gown falling open, the knot at my
middle coming undone. A year ago I
could have lifted him, wrestled them
both to the floor, who now, alone,

picks me up in his arms to turn me
over for another dose. In the car,
coming back, I wear a lap blanket,
bright red, my rings on one hand
swollen tight, gouging the skin,
and on the other taped to fit.
A young girl drives me, always face
ahead, but in the mirror
a bit of her, around the mouth,
her cheek, a little of one eye,
comes back to me. I have not yet
been able to define that look.

The Walk

Went for a walk this morning
down through the fields
saw blaze of color in wheat
saw color lie down in dirt stand up
in corn saw
three black birds rise up
out of a bush and fly
off eastward
stubbed on a rock that came as if
from out of nowhere
my toe
gasped grew tired cursed
at the earth how God damn big it is

house set back so tiny in the trees
the road behind me
decreasing decreasing
saw
farmers out on tractors
first dots
then growing nearer
larger
bigger tractors bigger farmers
saw
on their foreheads dust
sweat rust thought fear
and the eyes rolled back and out to the side
in search of rain
saw them go by heard them go by
big tires rolling around big hubs of wheels
cradling dust
the plow raised up behind
the way the pheasant lifts her tail
when strutting

Went for a walk this morning
out through the dew of the lawn
down past tree and shrub loved tree
loved shrub
saw all the wealth of my house and environs

saw how one world (the world of the hose and sprinkler)
gave way suddenly completely
to the new and other different older world
dirt dirt dirt dirt
miles and miles and the hot sun
land of the cattle gate and fence
land where the water comes down in a rush
goes whoosh
into the soil and the soil turns up
the same know-nothing face
land of wind
where the wind comes roaring and goes past
and everyone every thing bows
land of the rhino pig burrowing burrowing
out of the heat into soft mud
out of the sun into soft shade
a whole big bunch of them against the barn side
then fields
fields fields fields
and all the farmers home from the heat
fanning themselves perhaps
around a kitchen table
beer in cans
ice tea in tall glass beaded pitchers

I went for a walk this morning
leaving Crete
leaving my daughter sprawled in sleep
my son clenched
my wife in the disarray of sleep
and the dogs out back
penned in
noses over their paws
and the hard pawed walked on ground
the pig ground under them
straight south
walking a good clip
faster than the day before
out past the last few city houses
over the little bridge then up
the rise where the railroad tracks bunch
on the hill crest

then down
(though pausing once over the left side invitation
of the tracks, and all the foliage they lead back towards)
heading straight south
the fields coming up on both sides
corn to the left and
to the right side also corn
a half a mile to where the road stopped
hard
a field of corn

already the hot sun up and at me

Poetry

1

There is jam with the peanut butter.
There is no need for poetry.
And when the car starts the cold writhes.
I will not speak today of it.
I ask you, is there need for singing
in the tame world?
I do not think so.

We all live together quite happily
in a big house on a little hill.
The grass snoozes around us.
On it, in three clusters, the dogs
remark the falling or the rising day.
It falls, they bark.
It rises, and they bark.
Or they remark the wind.

From my window I can see the spot
where last year we built up the fire.
First with the old boxes, cartons,
and newspapers, then with the
scraps of wood, scarred furniture,
and then when the blaze was fierce,
there in the twilight we threw on
the poetry. It didn't catch.
This stuff won't burn you said,
it's not even good for that.

Jam with peanut butter,
and, in the cupboard, the right-made bread,
wheat and rye, with a handful of bran
mixed in. Honey, if we allow sugar that week,
crackers we fashioned ourselves—
the only people in this town to bake crackers.
And a big bowl of soup from the garden.
How do I write of the agony of lost days?

2

There is a reading tonight
in the Great Hall of the Sheldon Gallery.
The hall is filled with expectant listeners.
They have come, more or less,
from carefree Sunday afternoons,
warm from their dinners,
no scowls on their faces.
Some wear incredible coats with high fur collars.
Some traipse in in blue jeans,
others in Sunday suits.
They wink at the guards or smile or
look straight ahead,
then file in past where my son and daughter stand
handing out programs.
The seats fill up, the rows.
And then we close the great wood doors.
What is it will happen here?
What are we going to do?
And then Jack Collom steps up to the microphone.

3

I do not think this marks the extent
of poetry
or why we can have it.
There are those, I surmise,
for whom it is very costly,
both in what it is about
and how it discovers what it is about.
I like, as well, and respect
the theories, notions of getting going,
notions of loyalties to words,
to rhythms,
and the lost originals.
For everything augments poetry,
or serves to catalyze: I can
write as well of the ashes
as of the fire,
my mother a cripple at fifty-five,
my father remote for thirty years.
Or I can write of Jackie
with gold hair,
or I can kiss that hair.

4

And I prefer to kiss it.
Again I would kiss it
or fluff it up
or comb it down her small pale shoulders.
At night, when we sit together
in the big chair,
she tells me about her friends,
her teacher and her lunch,
all in a rapid succession,
the goulash of her day,
her plans,
her gargled words.
Today she's learning
the multiplication tables.
Last week she had finished with
subtractions.

5

What is poetry?
What is it for?
I have friends who write it,
perhaps they can say.
They are sometimes eager and sometimes still.
Sometimes we walk out down near the pond,
one of those friends and me,
and watch the frogs snap off the banks
like clothespins.
Or poke our fingers in the muskrat hole.
How low the water is today he says.
Look at the three crows,
or leads me to the homestead well,
a pipe up out of the ground
and still running.
Then we come back through the cut alfalfa,
I dropping to one knee to pick some up
and sniff it.
Belt buckle catch the sunlight,
dark shirt soak it up.
And the dogs about us like satellites,
whirling in the late day.

6

I have a mother for whom poetry
has never said a thing.
She tells me she does not retain language.
I am like a sink honey she says.
With the plug pulled.
When I talk to her of poetry
she looks through my beard to my face
or holds me on her lap
and feeds me strawberry custard.
It seems we are passionate about
different things.

I have a father for whom life is
nuts and bolts. When we speak together
he talks about snowmobiles or new tools,
and I, come far to visit with him briefly,
do not mention poetry or life.
He gets out a jar of olives,
and some beer. He has a big belly
and has taken to wearing banlon shirts
in order to exaggerate it.
A man beer made.
Drinking, he might even toast poetry.
And laugh.

7

There is a student who comes each Thursday
in the afternoon.
She sits in my office opposite my desk.
She is trying to write poetry.
We sit there together over her sheets.
I read some of her lines aloud,
she reads some lines.
Then poke at them.
She turns in the light of the room.
Far from her home, all the known things
of her life,
she tries to relax, and to keep me calm.
The last time she was here
she talked about her father
ten years dead.

It was in order to explain a line
in her poem,
but when she did not continue talking
I knew that for that day
it was enough.

8

For ten years I have been writing poetry.
For ten years she has been thinking about
her father,
how it was that he should die.
At first, she says,
it seemed like a betrayal.
He had said that I shouldn't worry,
that he would be back.
And then he did not come.
I feel in the room the presence
of some powerful emotion.
Her eyes grow deep, just as the bad poems
say.
And then she is gone for the day,
clutching her purse and hat.

9

Where did it all come from,
the poetry?
Each morning
big packages arrive
marked "poetry"
or "manuscript."
Fourth class mail.
Every week the books arrive,
New York, Wisconsin, everywhere.
Thin careful volumes or anthologies.
"These are really good,"
one blurb announces.
These, another shouts.
Each day I send my own poems out,
weighted and marked.
Return address and postage
for the coming back.

What are you doing
someone might ask,
some Tuesday or some afternoon.
Why, mailing poetry of course.
Or reading it,
or writing lectures on it for a class.

10

It *is* all lost in the translation
like they say.
The moving from out under your skin
to mine.
The shedding of light in dark places
discloses, to the viewer,
only his own world.
How well I do not see myself
here in my own pages.
How gracefully my daughter stood
and gave out programs on that Sunday past.

The Living World

The living world is a tissue stretched taut between trees in an abandoned park, the park full of rubber tires smoldering, broken bottles, and other dead things. The living world is a piece of paper blown curled up in the wind, the wind running breakneck down Canal Street, and now the rain. The living world is a shell out of which most of the meat has been eaten by embattled squirrels, the nub of meat left all that is left of the living world. The living world is at the corner of her mouth, not the corner where the red stain is, from the Kool Aid, but the other corner tucked in tight but still showing a glint of wetness. That is what the living world is. The living world is how at the edges of fields the light and the darkness meet and walk around each other the one trying to vanquish the other and the other trying to do the same. The living world starts at the tip of the bud on the branch in the April field and works backward down the fragile appendages down the stems down the longer larger thicker limb of the tree and into the main trunk, backwards always backwards to the roots. It stops when the living world coming upwards from the roots meets it somewhere in the center of the tree. The rest is what is dead. The living world is a stream carrying rain and dew gathered from the shanks of animals and dew from flowers and berries and rain dripping from leaves over the rocks. The rocks themselves are dead. The living world hastens and quickens, it struts about and coughs at the curtains just before they rise and just as they clink to the floor, as their lead weights strike the boards. The living world gets in the car next to you and pulls up her skirt just a little allowing the cool draft of the door to dry the sticky feeling down the backs of her thighs. It has been sitting all day in a waiting room waiting to begin, but now it is late and the doors shut and so you and the living world go home. You make a big dinner with wine and cheese. The living world slips into something comfortable. The living world will fall asleep on the couch and leave you with the dishes. The living world is afternoon, the sun with that sickly feeling about it, and you with that sickly feeling about you on account of the sun. The living world calls you late at night. The living world exerts its harsh voice through the phone wire into your mind. The living world has bad news for you on account of some cells somewhere some sickly things precarious above their own abyss having fallen to sleep in the pitch cold house having slipped down into darkness having set themselves on fire and so the living world is less. There begins the silence in your heart and the lump in your throat which signals that the living world has stopped telling you this and that tomorrow should the living world call you again it will be in a thinner voice, more remote, and with new images in it, or rather less of something and that something you. The living world is not for sale. The living world is morning come in over the doorstep and morning fogging the windows and morning in your aching joints and the scum covered tongue and the back which last night twisted by a giant, some vacuum in the dark, wakes into pain and wakes you to it. The living world is standing on the corner when you come to the corner. The living world extends its thumb. The living world will flag you down. The living world must stop you in your flight. You must pick up the living world or die. After having picked up the living world she will not get out of the car, he will not share with you the tedious driving, will not put his big pack in the back seat, will not look pretty as you intended, will not pass the time of day talking. The living world instead will pull a knife or pick its nose or shit on the seat next to you. My God how did you get yourself into such a predicament you will ask yourself, realizing that it is in vain to direct any questions to the living world. The living world was always there like this, friend at your elbow, teacher above you, janitor scrubbing the floors. The floor left wet and which you skid upon, that was the living world. The door which locked and locked you out, that was the living world. The letter you waited for but did not get, the slight change in your direction because of it, the definition forged there of betrayal, or just one sort of betrayal, that was the work of the living world. Friends have gone down into the living world. Friends have left their jobs and wandered off into the living world, never to be heard from again. In a small house by the sea the man who knows as much about the living world as anyone will not come to the door, will not write poems, or feed himself. He is trying to starve out the living world. He is trying to deny something to the living world. He is trying to ignore the living world. The living world will not cry out. Neither will it evaporate. The texture of your skin, the bad skin over the knuckles, the smooth skin under the ears, this is the texture of the living world. The petal of the tulip, so like the texture of the skin under the ear, this is the texture of the living world. This is that fragility which endures, out of which things continue to come and into rugged indifference mature. Likewise the icy glances and dark hates which populate our nightmares and our regrets, these are some of the dreams of the living world. You are in a boat, the living world all around you. It is called the sea. Throw yourself over the side, open your mouth and drink in the living world. You will gag on the living world. Or thrust your face forward into the living world of the wind. Flowers are opening, farmers are hushing their cows in from the fields. The living world dances in the dark barns. The living world eats beneath the hay mound. The carcass of the dead groundhog draws unto itself swarm after swarm of the living world. It is breakfast, it is time to eat from the living world, to select that which you like most this moment from the living world. A representative from the living world, the great incorporation of the living world inside you, will tell you what your appetite requires. Lift up your heart to the living world. Raise to your right temple the fingers held just so in a salute to the living world. Rinse from the sheets last night's love left, the joy and juice of the living world. Try to imagine another place.

Recovery

I went down lower than I thought
I could breathe, or stand, or turn in sleep,
I went down past bones, past faces
twisted in sleep, in dreams, in the pain
of being awake,
places crowded with misfortunes,
dense with hate, with anger, guilt,
faces hung down in defeat,
bodies shivering in hot sun,
whole rooms of reckless dreamers
breaking themselves on rocks,
or having their skin torn off by dogs
or other beasts,

and other rooms and other bodies,
some lovely to look upon, retaining
still a gloss, a filminess in which
the light lay lovingly, women
with powerful upturned breasts,
thighs sleek and strong,
beautiful faces,
and in all an emptiness of rooms,
of houses, places out of which
I had come not looking back

and then there were the bodies
of my dead, my own loved dead,
and of the living soon to die,
and these the most horrible, these
the worst by far, repulsive, mine,
in my own image, the fractured faces,
the shrunken forms, and now and then
one freshly killed, unchanged,
still with the shock of light
upon his face, but the darkness there too,

and thought, coming away from that
(how unendurable to have remained a moment
longer) what, is there no escaping,
is there no alternative but to pass,

as these, into the rooms to stay, onto
the tabletops and in strong light
be torn, be ravaged, or, in the long
corridors of empty chairs to sit
and wait eternity to shift, to crack,
and something other, sweeter, enter.

I passed, as you can see, from this
going and this thinking unto now,
this place, room in my own house,
among the gentle trees, the small
breeze tossing the garden flowers,
all the loveliness of a summer night,
and think, here, now, how unendurable
to hold one moment longer in this
wonderland, that I should be off,
carried by wind as some delicate seed
flies to a nowhere, unthinking,
or in some night-quick rain
gets washed down smacked by a drop
onto the soft soil and grows.

How terrible it is to be a mind,
to live in death or fearing death,
to live in love for fading things,
to be called, some midnight, up
from one's reveries, into the hard
wasteland of disaster, there to be
asked to speak, to dance, to turn
some phrase forward into light,
to reach out the selfsame human arm
that once was light as air
but now pulls down like a huge weight,
pulled by the earth's
terrible gravity.

Tonight I cradled my son in my arms.
I bent in a room of light and water
and scrubbed the skin flakes off his back,
where the sun had been,
directed the spray of the shower water
onto his small delicate skull,

saw the trim thin ankles, pale calves,
and the knees bruised and scabbed
from all the bike ride crashes and skids,
looked at his eyes full of the world's light,
of the mouth ajar with its own words,
and his own hands scrubbing his own
small chest and limbs,
and cursed for the claim of the darkness
on me, for the day of ruin,
for his own heart broken at my death,
cursed the lovely film that beckons us,
betrays us and all we love,
cursed all the dreams in their bright currency,
and my own stupidity,
all that does not look straight
into the face of the child, behind the dream,
cursed flesh, bone, and the nerves ringing,
cursed pain and selfishness,
the day of endings as well as our starting places,
all the fools we were and are and will be,
and if there be a one to hear or know or care,
cursed God for his mad trickery,
all this extravagance of dream
which is our lives lonely and inconsolable.

The Poet

I guess that I am finished as a poet.
I am no longer happy at writing.
Sitting in my chair at my desk I look around
I scratch my neck or pick the scabs on my head,
I try to look out of the window.
Most of the time I get up and leave the room
after but a few moments.
It is not an entirely uncomfortable feeling,
this leaving, this going away.
And this is why I must be finished as a poet.

I guess that I am all done being a poet.
Weeks have gone by and I have not written a poem.
Months have gone by and I have not had any urges.
Years, I think, have passed, since last I sent
any of my work off to Howard Moss at the New Yorker.

When I walk up the street past the mail box
I no longer shiver or sweat or get giddy.
When the phone rings I no longer dream an editor
will materialize at the other end and make me an offer.
When one of my students is reading a book in the hall
intently, really getting into it, I do not any more
hope that it is one of my books he or she is reading.
All of these bode ill for my continuing on much further
as someone interested in the writing and the reading
    of poems.

Sometimes late at night I wake from my otherwise sound
    sleep
and walk about inside my house.
Sometimes I walk the dark hallway down to what had
    formerly
been a place of much hustle and bustle, my office,
and stand there in the shadow of the desk,
the desk of delights I once called it.
Sometimes I rub my hand, I think my left one—the more
useless one—over the once warm now cool typewriter.
How wonderful it is not to be able to remember quite
    exactly
what it was I did here, or wanted to do, or dreamed of.

Then sometimes I go downstairs to the kitchen and make
    myself
a big ice cream soda.

The flowers this year were especially lovely.
I can't explain it, why it was so, I don't know enough
about flowers or plants or flowering trees and their bloom
    cycles
or their supposedly intimate relationship to the weather.
Were it as simple or complex as that I might leave it
at that but of course as you know I have been a poet
for years, the lost years I am beginning to call them,
and so I cannot trust myself that this year's flowers
are better, or that perhaps last year I was more busy,
more active, as a poet, and so did not notice them.

It is, I suppose, like being both dead and alive at the
same time. Perhaps other people experience this same thing
every day, but pass it off, or ignore it, or know it for
what it is, a visitation of insight, without trying to make
more of it than it is. Having been a poet I suppose
makes it impossible for me to pass anything off for what
    it is,
and even now, lapsed, failed, exhausted, and despising
poetry as I do, there is still the nervous after habit,
the residue of song as Marvin Bell once coined
for, I hope, quite another matter.

But I do, I do feel both dead and alive.
Having died, and having come back to the scene
of my living, the theatre of it,
and standing amidst the drama's props, like
someone on a guided tour of a famous place,
I look out from my safe and secure person at a world
obviously inert and trying to imagine what it once
    had been,
to laugh there, to grow feverish, to storm and pain,
to rant and dream, to work. And these
are the walls he looked about himself at,
and now I want to find some numbered item in the guide,
ah, pen set, a gift from his wife,
with which it is said he wrote the first draft of...

And now of course to step back out
into the just appearing edge of afternoon
turning the trees upon another part of the lawn
to shadow.

It is good, I think, essential, to give things up,
or to be given up by them.
There is the sudden hush which not only pervades
the whole place one is standing or sitting or lying
but which seems to begin within the very body and mind,
a grand impersonal stillness which is, finally,
deeply personal, a wholeness which is, finally,
a wholesomeness, not wanting anything, not knowing
what to do next or if anything will ever begin again
in terms of which we will be called upon to respond.
I think it is a condition of absolute health,
youth and vigor joined together with age and exhaustion,
where the foot dragging past and the nearly airborn future
come together in a quick click,
and the present spreads outward on and on forever
like the circle of wave set up by a pebble dropped
into the ocean. No
it is more motionless even than that, even than
that thin ridge of wave a thousand miles from the center.

Let's face it, poetry is a lot of work,
a lot of wishing.
Poetry is, oh shit, we had better go off to the library
to go on talking like this.
What I mean is, poetry (how the word seems strange now,
like my name spoken in church or underwater)
is an activity to be engaged in only by persons
whose lives are not their own, who can see some
hope in complaining or renaming.
Somehow, a couple of years or so ago, I ceased to be
a person of that variety.

Today, out in my yard, I sawed some limbs off a big tree
that had mysteriously toppled over in a light wind.
It had been a huge and lovely youthful looking tree,
with no apparent illness or sign of decay.
All the years we have lived here it was situated

between my property and that of George Beyer, my
neighbor to the south. For years
George and his son Doug and George's wife Marion
had stacked logs up against the south side of the tree,
using it as Robert Frost says of a living tree
in his famous poem "The Wood Pile." The tree
seemingly had taken no notice, seeming, I think now,
looking back and changing things as poets do,
somehow more itself for lodging against its roots
cut up versions of itself, like stanzas of poems, stacked
but in no organic arrangement.
Of course the stack of wood had helped hold the moisture
there against the roots on the south side, and this
combined with the great amount of water in the valley
between our two houses, caused the roots on that side
to rot or to stop holding.
A more than average wind, though nothing serious really,
blew the whole magnificent thing over
right across my driveway.
It has resulted, as you might guess, in a large amount
of work.
It has not resulted, which you may be surprised at,
in any real sense of loss or sadness in me.
Perhaps it is because the tree has gone on growing
as it always has, the leaves still fresh and firm,
and the birds still singing in the branches.
I did not even once have the occasion to think of the fall
of the tree, or rather its tilting,
as in any way connected or figuring or metaphoring
my own condition.
That is what I have enjoyed about not writing poetry.

Put it another way.
This is just another tree
that has fallen down in my yard.
All the years a tree was falling apparently
I was teaching myself through poems
what it was I thought and felt and ought to think
or feel, how they were problems, what their falling
had to do with me, the fallings (the lesser ones)
of their leaves, the irony of the thick heavy trunk
and the fragile delicate leaves, etc.,

so now that I have been through all that so many times
I can at last go out and stand next to the tree
without self consciousness or anxiety of any sort,
save for that attendant upon our relative sizes
and textures, etc., (a little thing when you come
to think ot it). I can work with my body
fully engaged, or nearly fully, my feet rooted
and not anxious to run back up the hill and climb
up into the tower room and write THE SONG OF
    THE TREE
or THE EVENT or THE HACKBERRY (it is a hackberry)
or THE BIG WIND.

Tonight I went out into the yard and walked around
without my shoes.
I walked on down towards the valley between my house
and George Beyer's, to the thick wet grassy section
which really belongs to me but which George has always
mowed, out of some unspoken understanding (funny how
    much
I see George now and think of him and like him
now that I am not writing poetry) and walked
as if without direction or aim or purpose up the valley
toward the little asparagus patch I have been giving myself
to more and more, on account of all my new freed time,
and felt—is it for the first time in my life here—
the deep coolness of the earth in that valley, the
almost frigid cold of the ground under the thick grass,
and the absolutely wonderful sensual pleasure of my feet
being touched by the blades of grass, both the cold green
ones and the dryer scratchier cut ones.
It was a marvelous experience, and nothing like it
did I ever have writing poetry.

I Will Rub My Arm

I will rub my arm.
I will rub through the first layer of dirt.
I will rub through the second layer.
I will sit in the tub and rub my arm with the cloth.
The steam will rise.
I will rub my arm down to the first layer of skin.
I will rub a red rose rush upon my arm.
I will rub until it goes away, the skin goes.
And then I will rub to the second layer.
I will rub my arm.
No one will stop me.

I will stand on the long line waiting for promotion, disease.
And I will rub my arm.
I will sit in a chair and read the lonely news,
of desperate men, of women in love,
and I will put my hand upon the skin of my arm.
In a grocery store pushing the cart
I will push it well, I will collect the edibles,
and I will rub my arm.
In the councils of the rich, reclining or at rest,
my arm will seem to me of great interest.

I will rub my arm.
I will laugh, then I will rub it.
It will be evening, and then a morning come.
It will be a worrisome time.
My arm will seem to me an inescapable.
Or it will be a good hot day, and children
in the street, or standing about joyfully,
and all the miseries in hiding,
and all the horrors pushed back like hair from a face,
but I will rub my arm.

In a swirl of conversation, two or three movements at
    work,
I will rub it.
In a place full of decent aspiring folks, some artists even,
when the drift is to silence, to the long drive back
in the dark,

I will be there with my arm for reassurance,
flesh that fades, tangible and fragile,
holding so much of my pain like a great ladle.

Dark or light
I will rub my arm.
Reach for the light, reach for a coke,
I will rub it.
For my children, born of this flesh,
even though I will never be able to tell them
all that I love,
or prove to them how terrible it was to live
through these years, in this body,
even though I will never be able to give
back to the world
a full deep measure of my engagement,
and many will think me foolish or vain,
at best a failure,
and few will know how much I love them,
I will not be annihilated,
I will not go dumb in a corner,
I will assert my presence, my soul, my flesh,
I will rub my arm.